Dogged Strength
within the Veil

D1553250

AFRICAN AMERICAN
RELIGIOUS THOUGHT AND LIFE

This series provides opportunity for African American scholars from a wide variety of fields in religion to develop their insights into religious discourse on issues that affect African American intellectual, social, cultural, and community life. The series focuses on topics, figures, problems, and cultural expressions in the study of African American religion that are often neglected by publishing programs centered on African American theology. The AARTL program of publications will bridge theological reflection on African American religious experience and the critical, methodological interests of African American religious studies.

SERIES EDITORS
ANTHONY B. PINN, Macalester College, St. Paul, Minnesota
VICTOR ANDERSON, Vanderbilt University, Nashville, Tennessee

Making the Gospel Plain
edited by Anthony B. Pinn

A Private Woman in Public Spaces
Barbara A. Holmes

Dark Salutations
Riggins R. Earl Jr.

Black Religion, Black Theology
edited by David Emmanuel Goatley

Dogged Strength within the Veil
Josiah Ulysses Young III

Dogged Strength within the Veil

AFRICANA SPIRITUALITY AND THE
MYSTERIOUS LOVE OF GOD

Josiah Ulysses Young III

TRINITY PRESS INTERNATIONAL
A Continuum imprint
HARRISBURG • LONDON • NEW YORK

Trinity Press International, P.O. Box 1321, Harrisburg, PA 17105

Trinity Press International is a member of the Continuum International Publishing Group.

Cover art: *Hanos,* Gedewon Makonnen, 1975. Copyright Réunion des Musées Nationaux/Art Resource, NY.

Cover design: Brenda Klinger

Library of Congress Cataloging-in-Publication Data

Young, Josiah U. (Josiah Ulysses)
    Dogged strength within the veil : Africana spirituality and the mysterious love of God / Josiah Ulysses Young III.
       p. cm. – (African American religious thought and life)
    Includes bibliographical references and index.
    ISBN 1-56338-346-2 (pbk.)
    1. African Americans – Religion. 2. Spiritual life – Christianity.
I. Title. II. Series.
BR563.N4 Y685 2003
 230′.089′96073 – dc21

                            2003004348

Printed in the United States of America

03 04 05 06 07 08   10 9 8 7 6 5 4 3 2 1

In memory of my cousin
Ralph Loundermon
killed within the veil in Vietnam, 1969

Death is swallowed up in victory

Contents

Part Four
THE MYSTERIOUS LOVE OF GOD
Burning through the Veil

Acknowledgments

Anthony Pinn graciously invited me to submit a proposal for African American Religious Thought and Life, the series he and Victor Anderson edit for Trinity Press International. I am grateful to Henry Carrigan for guiding my proposal through the channels at Trinity and patiently awaiting my delivery of the manuscript, which just made the deadline. I am also indebted to Professor Cain Felder of Howard University, who published an essay I wrote entitled "Dogged Strength within the Veil" in the *Journal of Religious Thought,* which he edits. He thus helped me to work out a few of the ideas on which this book is based. Most of my colleagues at Wesley Theological Seminary were very positive about this project when I shared three chapters of it during a faculty study session. Wesley's ongoing commitment to academic freedom and to theological diversity makes for an excellent environment in which to work. I also want to thank my students, especially those who took the class that launched this book, "African-American Spirituality as a Literary Tradition."

Finally, my deepest appreciation goes to my family. My wife, Pamela Monroe, helped me get the manuscript into readable shape; our sessions helped me see what I was trying to do so that much of the dross was burned away. My daughter, Thandi, put up with countless afternoons of "*Shhhh* — just let me finish this sentence, and then we'll play," while my six-foot, six-inch son, who has become quite the scholar and a talented basketball player, displayed his understanding too, borne from years of experience with his dad's vocation.

Part One

Introduction

Chapter 1

"Ever at Thy Glowing Altar"
The Problem

> Father, Son, and Holy Ghost,
> So I make an idle boast;
> Jesus of the twice-turned cheek,
> Lamb of God, although I speak
> With my mouth thus, in my heart
> Do I play a double part.
> Ever at Thy glowing altar
> Must my heart grow sick and falter.
> — COUNTEE CULLEN[1]

Most of us who are baptized and descended from black Africans are American Christians because slave owners imposed Christianity (i.e., the Religion) on our ancestors. Granted, the first generation of Africans who survived the Middle Passage, a journey pertinent to my concern for Africa today, held on to what they could salvage of their African religions and so refused the Religion. Nonetheless, their subjugated and intimidated descendants yielded over time to the pressures of slavery-upholding evangelicals.

In his *White over Black*, historian Winthrop Jordan describes the process through which the chattelized, the American-born progeny of the Africans, became the Christianized. According to Jordan, colonial Protestantism upheld "a conception of the morphology of conversion" that advocated scrutiny of the inner workings of the one to be converted. For Jordan, Protestants' focus on the cultivation of a piety beyond church liturgy, and thus the necessity for the faithful to have a direct relationship with God in accordance with *sola scriptura*, meant that church authority carefully monitored conversion to Christianity. In the case of the blacks, ecclesial supervision sublated the black body, itself equated with libidinousness and the aberrant, to Anglo-Saxon paternity. According to Jordan, this view that whites could convert blacks

only painstakingly and bit by bit — that conversion was "a process rather than an act" — upheld both the commitment to white
supremacy and the view that Christianizing slaves was akin to
"tribal adoption."[2]

Although the Great Awakening lowered such high standards and
thus accelerated the evangelists' Christianization of blacks, the inferior status of blacks remained very much in force. The nascent
Anglo-American state and the Religion that blessed it demanded
that blacks obey their masters or forgo salvation. Emancipation
did little to change that master-slave dialectic, for the descendants of the enslaved Africans were hardly as saved, and thus
hardly as American, as their white counterparts. From the post-
Reconstruction period until today, American Protestantism has
been itself inextricable from the problem of racism in America, so
much so that many blacks hold that Christianity is the white man's
religion.

William Jones's *Is God a White Racist?*, for instance, calls Christianity "Whiteanity." Jones finds especially bothersome the claims
that blacks transformed the "white man's religion" to fit their
needs and that the black experience was thus "made less onerous" because of this blackenized religion.[3] "Less onerous"? Jones
finds no evidence to that effect. For Jones, it is rather the case that
the Religion is "a carrier of oppression's virus...a yet undetected
and unidentified Typhoid Mary."[4] According to Jones, neither the
black church nor blacks' overall Christianization has had "positive value" as an instrument of liberation. It is rather the case that
the black church has been captive to a "form of misreligion that
[fulfills] a vital role in keeping blacks oppressed."[5]

Anthony Pinn, whose book *Why Lord?* is in Jones's iconoclastic
tradition, holds that cultural resources within the black community, blues and rap music, for example, are far more liberating
for blacks than is Christianity. For Pinn, Christianity hamstrings
the struggle against white supremacy in coercing blacks to capit-
ulate to theistic, or nationalistic, imperatives — which is Jones's
point precisely. According to Pinn, denial of the existence of God
frees the freedom-famished black "from the dangerous doctrinal
and theological obligations inherent in theistic responses to suffering."[6] Eschewing "theistic responses" for a "strong humanism"
grounded in African Americans' cultural resources, the black community discovers an intense loyalty to itself "above any allegiance
to theological categories and platitudes."[7]

African American ethicist Victor Anderson criticizes the Religion in terms of what he calls "ontological blackness" — the penumbra as it were of Christian theology since the Atlantic slave trade. Ontological blackness is in part an "aesthetic consciousness," "a mirroring of the neoclassicist moral consciousness that was...developed in the European Enlightenment and Romantic heroic self-understanding."[8] Yet ontological blackness is also anchored in privation, constructed "on the dialectical structures that categorical racism and white racial ideology bequeathed to African American intellectuals (notwithstanding its claims for privileging black sources)."[9] As a result, Anderson argues, the black Christian, as exemplified in black theology, "remains an alienated being whose mode of existence is determined by crisis, struggle, resistance, and survival — not thriving, flourishing, or fulfillment."[10]

W. E. B. Du Bois, Toni Morrison, and James Baldwin deepen the view that North American Protestantism holds blacks captive to an ontology that negates them. Although I will discuss their perspectives in detail later in this book, I want to provide a few examples of their outlook now.

Toni Morrison argues that white Protestant America has from its inception defined itself at the expense of blacks — chattelized Africans whose bondage and pigment raised white American identity from bestial nature. For Morrison, neither the churches nor their theologies have been free from that racist dependency: "How could one speak of profit, economy, labor, progress, suffragism, *Christianity*...without having as a referent...the presence of Africans and their descendants"?[11] "In what public discourse does the reference to black people not exist"?[12] Unquestionably, the reference "is there in theological discourse...is inextricable from the definition of Americanness — from its origins on through its integrated or disintegrating twentieth-century self."[13]

James Baldwin's essay "Everybody's Protest Novel" provides a genealogy of that reference. He writes of "the African, exile, pagan," who, "hurried off the auction block and into the fields, fell on his knees before that God in Whom he must now believe; who had made him, but not in His image. This tableau, this impossibility," writes Baldwin, "is the heritage of the Negro in America: *Wash me*, cried the slave to his Maker, *and I shall be whiter...than snow!* For black is the color of evil; only the robes of the saved are white."[14] Baldwin's tableau exemplifies Africana philosopher Lewis Gordon's view that "if God is white, then the situation of blackness becomes that of eternal damnation. It would mean that the Eternal Eyes that constitute the Eternal Third from whose perspective black bodies are seen as what they are would be an antiblack perspective. Antiblackness would literally become *the natural condition;* it would be *the way things are* and *the way things will be.* Blacks would be essentially damned."[15]

In his *Dusk of Dawn,* specifically the chapter entitled "The White World," W. E. B. Du Bois argues that the "Christianity of the Gospels" has undergone quite a change in the West. Du Bois writes: "Europe had followed the high, ethical dream of a young Jew but twisted that ethic beyond recognition to any end that Europe wanted. If that end was murder, the 'Son of God went forth to war!' If that end was slavery, God thundered, 'Cursed be Canaan,' and Paul echoed 'Servants obey your masters!' If poverty was widespread and seemingly inevitable, Christ was poor and alms praise-worthy."[16] Mimicking that transmogrified Christianity to criticize its racism in the United States, Du Bois writes: "In order to defend America and make an efficient, desirable country, we must have authority and discipline. This may not sound like the Good Will of the Christian but at bottom, it is. There is no use pretending any longer that all men are equal. We know perfectly well that Negroes, Chinamen, Mexicans and a lot of others who are presuming to exercise authority in this country are not our equals."[17] It is no surprise, then, that Du Bois would write in *Darkwater: Voices from within the Veil* that blacks have been compelled to notice well "the utter failure of white religion. We have curled our lips in something like contempt as we have witnessed glib apology and weary explanation. Nothing of the sort deceived us. A nation's religion is its life, and as such white Christianity is a miserable failure."[18]

In his final memoirs, Du Bois makes bitterly clear his suspicion that Christianity serves inhumane theistic ends — or as Anthony Pinn has put it, "dangerous doctrinal and theological obligations inherent in theistic responses to [black] suffering."[19] In his early nineties, Du Bois wrote what may have been his parting shot regarding the Religion:

> I have long faced the inevitability of death and not tried to dodge the thought. In early manhood I wrote: "I saw a mother, black and seared and iron-haired, who had watched her boy through college, for men to jeer at and discourage and tempt until he sought women and whiskey and died. She crept on a winter's Sunday into a Cathedral of St. John

> The Divine and crouched there where a comfortable red and
> yellow angel sat sunning her ample limbs 'To keep the Mem-
> ory of Obadiah James Green' — a stock-gambler. And there
> she rested while the organ warbled the overture to *Der Fei-
> schutz*, and the choir asserted 'My Jesus! As thou wilt.' The
> priest intoned: 'Come unto Me all ye that labor and are heavy
> laden and I will give you rest! For my yoke is easy and my
> burden light.' And the window-angel moved a fat wing and
> murmured: 'except niggers!' "[20]

Even at the brink of death, Du Bois thought that Christianity qua
the white man's religion nullified him.

Although these arguments are persuasive and historically sound,
I don't believe Christianity can be reduced to the white man's religion. If the New Testament is the first-century source of Christian
identity, it is hard to make that Testament identical with a modern
appropriation of it. What Du Bois has pointed out bears repeating: "Europe had followed the high, ethical dream of a young Jew
but twisted that ethic beyond recognition to any end that Europe
wanted" — including the enslavement of Africans. That fact suggests that John's Christ, who from the beginning is the Wisdom of
creation, and Mark's Christ, who is forsaken by his Father, signify
a spirituality quite different from "Whiteanity" and its resentful
shadow, "ontological blackness." Certainly William Jones has argued persuasively that such a distinction does not of itself mean
that the gospel is a hallowed resource for black liberation. Still,
it is difficult to claim that Mark's Christ's God is the apotheosis
of Jones's "white racist" or a substantiation of Pinn's critique of
white theism. Indeed, Jones makes that point in his own way as
he removes "God's overruling sovereignty from human history"
in order to emphasize "the functional ultimacy of man."[21] Jones
thus advances a "theory of human history in which the interplay
of human power centers and alignments is decisive. In this context, racism is traced, causally, to human forces."[22] On that basis,
Jones's problem and that of the others — and my own — has more
to do with the racist interpretation of the gospel rather than the
gospel itself.

That is very significant to me. Certain Christian theologians
hold that the gospel's crucified and resurrected Son of Man is
the *human* God through whom *all* persons and things have been
made. As a christological term tied to wisdom and new creation,
"human" transcends "races" and cultures establishing their goal.

If that is true — if humankind will be without racist hierarchy, by virtue of God's Wisdom — then the critique of the white man's religion — that is, Whiteanity — identifies a hateful distortion of the gospel, one unbelievably hostile to the resurrection from the dead. Can "oppression's virus" be the promise of that triumph over death? No. A radical eschatological perspective enables one to take Jones's perspicacity to heart as a hermeneutic of suspicion without assuming that the object of his critique is the gospel or that all Christian theologians are devotees of the Religion.

Indeed, Jürgen Moltmann, making much of Mark's gospel, is troubled by the fact that Europeans and Euro-Americans are *in charge of* the production of Christian meaning. Their "theory of Christianity" is little different from Hegel's universal history, in which "the knowledge of being" apprehends "its own time in thoughts." Moltmann raises an excellent question in regard to such an ontology: If it is "only possible when what is real is rational, so such a theory of Christianity in terms of world history is possible only when what is real is Christian. But what is 'real?'" And what is Christian? Indeed, this ontology's nullification of African people exacts an exorbitant price from them if universal history is truly Christian, namely "that of ignoring the 'dialectic of the Enlightenment'... in the modern world, the misery of the modern age characterized by the names of Auschwitz and Hiroshima, and the conflicts which modern capitalism and the white man have produced."[23] Indeed, the Enlightenment dialectic sanctioned the extensive slave trade between Africa and North America. As European philosophers began to celebrate the white man's noetic maturity during "the time of European classicism and romanticism[,] the slave revolts began in the United States. In this perspective the egocentric particularism is dissolved in more universal relationships."[24] The fact remains, however, that this "egocentric particularism" has been so strong as to render both "the problem of the color line"[25] and the crimes against African humanity invisible for many theologians until today.

What does it mean, then — to borrow Moltmann's question — "that at the time of the Enlightenment, Europe was implicated in the vast slave trade between Africa and North America?"[26] It means to me that the Enlightenment dialectic has designated Africa as the necessary servant of the "white man," the "form of God." According to Hegel, the "form of God" is related to "Spirit" in the Christian state — England, for instance, or Germany. For Hegel, the Ultimate has become conscious of itself through the state, and especially through its "Philosophy," "Religion," and "Art." For Hegel, "[Art] advances farther into the realm of the actual and sensuous than Religion. In its noblest walk it is occupied with representing, not indeed the Spirit of God, but certainly the Form of God; and in its secondary aims, that which is divine and spiritual generally."[27] Given the Enlightenment dialectic, the form of God is in effect the master, the white, not the slave, the black.

For Hegel, "slavery is itself a phase of advance from the merely isolated sensual existence — a phase of education — a mode of becoming participant in a higher morality and the culture connected with it. Slavery is in and for itself *injustice*, for the essence of humanity is *Freedom;* but for this man must be matured. The gradual abolition of slavery is therefore wiser and more equitable than its sudden removal."[28] In other words, African slaves have become "free," that is, Christianized and Europeanized, by virtue of their instruction by a "higher morality and culture" embodied by the English, "who have done most for abolishing the slave-trade and slavery."[29]

That the English colonized huge portions of the Continent of the people they had enslaved thus made perfect sense from the perspective of Hegel's dialectic. As African philosopher V. Y. Mudimbe put it, the religious and aesthetic understanding of being, and thus of freedom — that is, "Spirit," as found in Hegel's *The Philosophy of History* — upholds "the inherent superiority of the white race, and . . . the necessity for European economies and structures to expand to 'virgin areas' of the world."[30] In colonizing Africa, Europe designated it as little more than the space in which the "form of God" could build on the traces of his intellectual concerns. That "freedom," however, has devastated Africa and taken a toll on Europe too.

Du Bois has examined that devastation in terms of the Berlin Conference of 1884. Organized through the Machiavellian cunning of King Leopold of Belgium, the Berlin Conference allocated huge portions of Africa to European states — France, Germany, England. According to Du Bois, the conference "was reported to be an act of civilization against the [Arab] slave trade."[31] It was in truth a commitment to exploit Africa for the sole good of Europe.[32] "The cost of this exploitation was enormous. The colonial system caused ten times more deaths than actual war."[33] Adam Hochschild's book *King Leopold's Ghost* reports that King Leopold's hold over the Congo alone is responsible for the extermination of approximately ten million people between 1885 and 1924.[34] The dead were not victims of calculated genocide, but they were victims of a crime against humanity nonetheless: "Like the slave dealers who raided Africa for centuries before them, Leopold's men were looking for labor. If, in the course of their finding and using that labor, millions of people died, that to them was incidental."[35] And so was "the German extermination of the Herero people in southwest Africa during Hitler's childhood."[36] One could well assert that "Auschwitz was the modern industrial application of a policy of extermination on which European world domination had long since rested."[37] Du Bois put it this way: "There was no Nazi atrocity — concentration camps, wholesale maiming and murder, defilement of women or ghastly blasphemy of childhood — which the Christian civilization of Europe had not long been practicing against colored folk in all parts of the world in the name of and for the defense of a Superior Race born to rule the world."[38] Virtually invisible in the Christian theodicies of the First World, those atrocities were in effect the legacies of the Middle Passage.

Du Bois writes of "the religious paradox: the contradiction between the Golden Rule and the use of force to keep human beings in their appointed places; the doctrine of the White Man's Burden and the conversion of the heathen, faced by the actuality of famine, pestilence, and caste."[39] He thought that ugly contradiction "distorted the development of Europe" and was rooted in the Middle Passage. He writes: "One of the chief causes which . . . distorted the development of Europe was the African slave trade, and we have tried to re-write its history and to make it occupy a much less important place in the world's history than it deserves. . . . The result of the African slave trade and slavery on the European mind and culture was to degrade the position of labor and the respect for humanity as such."[40]

One can understand why Toni Morrison argues with such fury and anguish:

> Slavery broke the world in half, it broke it in every way. It broke Europe. It made them into something else, it made them slave masters, it made them crazy. You can't do that for hundreds of years and it not take a toll. They had to dehumanize, not just the slaves but themselves. They have had to reconstruct everything in order to make that system appear true. It made everything in World War II possible. It made World War I necessary. Racism is the word that we use to

encompass all this. The idea of scientific racism suggests some serious pathology.[41]

One also can understand why James Baldwin writes that "the South African coal miner, or the African digging for roots in the bush, or the Algerian mason working in Paris, not only have no reason to bow down before...Westminster Abbey, or the cathedral at Chartres: they have, once these monuments intrude on their attention, no honorable access to them. Their apprehension of this history cannot fail to reveal to them that they have been robbed, maligned, and rejected: to bow down before that history is to accept that history's arrogant and unjust judgement."[42]

More than two decades before Baldwin penned those words, Du Bois had already put the situation in historical perspective: "Just as Europe lurched forward to a new realization of beauty, a new freedom of thought and religious belief, a new demand by laborers to choose their work and enjoy its fruit, uncurbed greed rose to seize and monopolize the uncounted treasure of the fruit of labor.... There came a new doctrine of universal labor: mankind were of two sorts — the superior and the inferior." According to Du Bois, this dialectic meant that "no equality was possible or desirable for 'darkies.' In line with this conviction, the Christian Church, Catholic and Protestant, at first damned the heathen blacks with the 'curse of Canaan,' then held out hope of freedom through 'conversion,' and finally acquiesced in a permanent status of human slavery."[43]

Du Bois, Morrison, and Baldwin personify a certain spirituality. By that I mean a truthful expression in quest of justice, which brings to mind the conceptualization of Emmanuel Levinas, the popular Lithuanian-born Jewish philosopher, of the *face* — an important metaphor in this book. The "face" pertains to the "third person," the Other beyond the alterity of the I-Thou relation. In his *Otherwise Than Being*, Levinas writes that "the third party [person] is other than the neighbor, but also another neighbor, and also a neighbor of the Other, and not simply his fellow."[44] The third person's face tells a story, narrates an alterity, usually excluded from the I-Thou relation. For instance, if that relation pertains to the European Christian and the European Jew, the black person who expresses him- or herself as Du Bois does, or Morrison or Baldwin, is the third person: the *face* that ruptures the Religion qua the I-Thou relation. The third party thus "introduces a contradiction" that had been invisible in a dialogue that "until then went in one direction."[45] By virtue of his or her dogged strength, the third-person's face raises the matter of responsibility for all humankind with an unimpeachable authority: "What do I have to do with justice? A question of consciousness. Justice is necessary, that is, comparison, coexistence, contemporaneousness, assembling, order, thematization, the visibility of faces...a copresence on an equal footing as before a court of justice."[46] A bit of Countee Cullen's poem "Heritage" comes to mind:

> Quaint, outlandish heathen gods
> Black men fashion out of rods,
> Clay, and brittle bits of stone,
> In a likeness like their own,
> My conversion came high-priced;
> I belong to Jesus Christ,
> Preacher of humility;
> Heathen gods are naught to me.
>
> Father, Son, and Holy Ghost,
> So I make an idle boast;
> Jesus of the twice-turned cheek,
> Lamb of God, although I speak
> With my mouth thus, in my heart
> Do I play a double part.
> Ever at Thy glowing altar
> Must my heart grow sick and falter.[47]

My conversion came high-priced; / I belong to Jesus Christ, / Preacher of humility; / Heathen gods are naught to me. As if "before a court of justice," the third person's "face" questions the Religion from his or her American beginnings and asks, *What do I have to do with justice?* A question of consciousness, that, to quote the poet, ponders *"Quaint, outlandish heathen gods, / Black men fashion out of rods, / Clay, and brittle bits of stone, / In a likeness like their own."* Aren't those artifacts nullified by the "glowing altar" because of what Levinas calls a certain "ipseity," a powerful solipsism, "an existence *for itself* ... as the 'famished stomach that has no ears' "?[48] Yet the face, veiled by the ipseity in question and beneath the African mask — quaint, outlandish, heathen — asserts itself.

During a visit to New York City's Museum of Natural History decades ago, I was startled by an African mask, one made by the

Bambara people of West Africa. Hindsight reveals that I, to borrow from Levinas, was moved by the insinuation of a face beyond
the plasticity of the object — which virtually shut out everything
else for me in the museum. Thereafter I began to study the works
of people such as Dominique Zahan. In his book *La dialectique du
verbe chez les Bambara* (*The Bambara's Dialectic of the Verbe*),
Zahan presents the Bambara conviction that humankind differs
from other animals by virtue of language, *la parole*, which links us
essentially to God. *Dieu est, par excellence, la parole:* God *is* the
(spoken) word; and God's *verbe* works in Bambara society, such
that one can say that human labor, which "makes" millet grow, is
God's *verbe*. For the Bambara, human beings are distinguished by
their speech much in the same way that lions are distinguished by
their manes or antelopes by their tails.[49] In other words, humans
have neither tail (*queue*) nor mane (*crinière*) — are neither lion nor
antelope — but take their place in the cosmos by way of the word
of their mouths. Human speech in all its organizing power and fecundity is like the antelope's tail or the lion's mane — comparable
to a physical element that identifies, as in completes, a being. The
word "finishes" (*parachève*) the human being, accounts for his or
her distinctiveness in the material and therefore the spiritual do-
main.[50] Behind the mask, say in the shape of the antelope, is thus
no brute sensibility but a spirituality in truth, which one ought not
caricature. It is utterly false that "in Negro life the characteristic
point is the fact that consciousness [had] not yet attained to the
realization of any substantial objective existence — as for example,
God, or Law — in which the interest of man's volition is involved
and in which he realizes his own being."[51] It is hardly the case
that the Bambara spirituality that made me do a double take was
free from inhumanity. The Bambara (of modern-day Mali) played
a major role in supplying the Atlantic slave trade. Still, Bambara
society is not to be discarded as a voided state.

In his book *The Idea of Africa*, V. Y. Mudimbe writes that "the
worked object [e.g., the mask] is, in effect, a live memory, reproducing, in its own successive concrete images, its conceptual and
cultural destiny, which, often and explicitly, is a testimony to a will
to remember or to *forget* certain things. To reinvest worked ob-
jects with their own past from the context of their own society
is, indeed, to revive the historical activity and the reactiveness of
a culture with its motions and exemplary beauty."[52] To revive the
historical activity and the reactiveness of a culture with its motions

and exemplary beauty is to ask with the third persons, the nullified ancestors: Was the great blessing of the Middle Passage the
Religion that substantiates Lewis Gordon's insight that "the black
and white desire a white god on a pre-reflective level primarily because God *means* whiteness"?[53] If so, no wonder "heathen gods are
naught to me" — no wonder Gordon writes that "only the white
can reflect upon himself as being pre-reflectively linked to God in
his essential feature of value: his whiteness."[54]

The celebrated European theologian Wolfhart Pannenberg echoes
Gordon's observation. Pannenberg writes that "the future of God's
Kingdom, its saving of this world, is related to this world in an as-
sertive and positive manner. This means that for the sake of the
kingdom of God, the Church must resist the temptation to disdain *the* social and cultural heritage. A disdain for, and wasting
of, this heritage is usually connected with revolutionary move-
ments. We should not be reckless with history."[55] But how universal
is this social and cultural heritage? And who is revolutionary?
Who wastes Pannenberg's heritage? Baldwin? Du Bois? Morrison?
Levinas? Moltmann? Pannenberg's sense that the future of God's
kingdom is related positively to Western civilization is not true
for many African people. His Religion suggests that our African
"memories" are unresurrectionable, are "incompatible with God's
presence."[56]

The legacy of the wedding of chattelization and Christianization troubles me: *Father, Son, and Holy Ghost, / So I make an idle
boast; / Jesus of the twice-turned cheek, / Lamb of God, although
I speak / With my mouth thus, in my heart / Do I play a double part. / Ever at Thy glowing altar / Must my heart grow sick
and falter.* Am I really thanking the master for enslavement, for
"freedom," when I approach the communion rail? That problem,
which has given rise to this book, directs me and hopefully others
to the third-person "face." As I have pointed out, "face" signifies
the integrity of a spirituality through which the dark progenitors —
"Heritage," if you will — melt through the oppressive Religion and
its double standard. Du Bois's anecdote set out earlier comes back
to haunt me:

> "A comfortable red and yellow angel sat sunning her ample
> limbs 'To keep the Memory of Obadiah James Green' — a
> stock-gambler. And there [the third person] rested while the
> organ warbled the overture to *Der Feischutz*, and the choir
> asserted 'My Jesus! As thou wilt.' The priest intoned: 'Come

unto Me all ye that labor and are heavy laden and I will
give you rest! For my yoke is easy and my burden light.' And
the window-angel moved a fat wing and murmured: 'except
niggers!' "

In faltering at the altar when upset by the radical distinction between the gospel and what the New World has done with it, I hear
Bambara slaves murmur, "like a thousand wings beating on the
air."[57] They trouble my mind and make it increasingly difficult to
play a "double part" before the altar. Jones, Du Bois, Morrison,
Baldwin, Moltmann, Levinas, and others steady my spirit. I cannot burn through the Religion without their faces, their compelling
criticisms of hateful speculation.

Chapter 2

Burning through
the Plastic Image
The Approach

This *mode* [face] does not consist in figuring as a theme under my gaze, in spreading itself forth as a set of qualities forming an image. The face of the Other at each moment destroys and overflows the plastic image it leaves me, the idea existing to my own measure and to the measure of its *ideatum* — the adequate idea. It does not manifest itself by the invented "qualities," but . . . *expresses itself.*   — EMMANUEL LEVINAS[1]

To flush out the significance of this book's title, *Dogged Strength within the Veil: Africana Spirituality and the Mysterious Love of God*, in relation to the problem of the Religion just introduced, I would like to discuss the four motifs — "dogged strength," "the veil," "the mysterious love of God," and "Africana spirituality."

Two Warring Ideals in One Dark Body: Dogged Strength Alone Keeps It from Being Torn Asunder

I take "dogged strength" from this controversial sentence in "Of Our Spiritual Strivings," the lead essay in Du Bois's seminal *The Souls of Black Folk:* "One ever feels his two-ness — an American, a Negro; two souls, two thoughts, two unreconciled strivings; two warring ideals in one dark body, whose dogged strength alone keeps it from being torn asunder."[2] Without dogged strength, blacks would be vanquished by the hateful ways their homeland mortifies them in privileging the "form of God." With dogged strength, one manages his or her double-consciousness without being torn apart from the inside out.

However, political scientist Adolph Reed and ethicist Victor Anderson find that blacks' usage of Du Bois's double-consciousness is parochial. Reed holds that too many blacks idealize "twoness" as the essence of African American life. Reed finds that such an essentialist view as peculiar as double-consciousness was not unique to Du Bois but "prominent among fin-de-siècle American intellectuals."[3] According to Reed, the popular notion that double-consciousness has sprung of necessity from black American experience alone depends "on a notion of linear tradition that approaches discrete subjects principally as artifacts of the lineage," as icons of an essentialism that "reifies and animates ideas."[4] For Reed, such puppetry is "blind to the importance of changing social contexts in the constitution of ideas and their meanings."[5] Reed thinks the usage of double-consciousness by black scholars — such as Harvard's Henry Louis Gates — signifies today "the nostalgic yearning for a mythical past of organic racial community that both mediates petit bourgeois status anxiety and eases accommodation to rightward shift in the ideological context within which incremental political agendas and prevailing models of respectable middle-class opinion are constructed."[6]

I see no reason, though, for such "anxiety" to typify all for whom double-consciousness has relevance today. Has Du Bois's double-consciousness no relevance in the twenty-first century apart from blacks' alleged vapid striving to attain bourgeois-American respectability? Must all remembrances of the slave community — as in the so-called "mythical past of organic racial community" — placate the Protestant "Spirit"? Is there nothing to the claim that a certain appropriation of double-consciousness enables one to overcome that "Spirit"? Barring Reed's claim that Du Bois virtually abandoned double-consciousness in later years, for I have been unable to find evidence of that, I agree with Reed that Du Bois's double-consciousness must be situated in the context of his life. But why would the dynamism of Du Bois's history and the dissonance between the writing Thou and the reading I divest "Of Our Spiritual Strivings" of a certain traditional import, of relevance for today? Why not say that the "canonical" implications of "two souls, two thoughts, two unreconciled strivings" indicate the persistence of resistance to a nullifying Religion? Until today, blacks have faced the ramifications of Hegel's hegemonic view that "the German nations, under the influence of Christianity, were the first to attain the consciousness, that man, as man, is free: that it is the *freedom* of Spirit which constitutes its essence."[7] Construed in terms of Protestantism, then, Africans' enslavement in the Americas has been deemed as salvific, for there alone, in the church, have the Africans' progeny known freedom. The state itself has upheld that freedom in coercing blacks to renounce the antithesis of the state and the Religion — the African heritage. One would lay that heritage "aside in Devotion — a state of mind" done with "the limited and particular."[8] As I have pointed out, the master's Art, his "plastic activity" (remember Du Bois's "fat-winged angel") clinches the matter as "it is occupied with representing... the form of God."[9] The black who acknowledges that icon as God's form is thus spiritualized through the Religion and Art and Science of the master. In the obedient black, the "Spirit *knows itself*," appreciates its own nature — makes "itself *actually* that which it is *potentially*."[10]

Because of that "Spirit," however, blackness or Africanness is not truly at home in the United States of America and its historic religious tradition. For that reason alone, Du Bois's appropriation of "twoness" has a certain ancestral import that is hardly passé. The question that begins "Spiritual Strivings" and introduces the concept "double-consciousness," itself integral to "dogged strength," endures:

> Between me and the other world there is ever an unasked question: unasked by some through feelings of delicacy; by others through the difficulty of rightly framing it. All, nevertheless, flutter round it. They approach me in a half-hesitant sort of way, eye me curiously or compassionately, and then, instead of saying directly, How does it feel to be a problem? they say, I know an excellent colored man in my town; or, I fought at Mechanicsville; or, Do not these Southern outrages make your blood boil?... To the real question, How does it feel to be a problem? I answer seldom a word.[11]

Nearly a century after the publication of *The Souls of Black Folk*, Toni Morrison provides insight into the question "How does it feel to be a problem?" by writing, "I hate when people come into my presence and become white. I'd just been elected to the American Academy of Arts and Letters and a man whom I used to read in anthologies came up to me and said, 'Hello, welcome to the Academy.' Then his third sentence was about his splendid black housekeeper. This little code saying, 'I like black people or I know one,' is humiliating for me — and should have been for him."[12]

James Baldwin provides insight, itself borne from his dogged strength, that reveals the problematic relation between blacks and whites. According to Baldwin, their association depends on what the white cannot say to the black and what the black will not say to the white, and one of them is lying in wait for what is unsaid; one of them "is listening." They are conspirators, argues Baldwin, not friends. For such vigilance, in which one "is listening, to all those things, precisely, which are not being said," is hardly *friendship:* "The intensity of this attention can scarcely be described as the attention one friend brings to another. If one...is listening, both...are plotting, though, perhaps, only one...knows it. Both...may be plotting to escape, but, since very different avenues appear to be open to each...[they] are plotting...escape from each other."[13] Baldwin thus unveils the racialized duplicity common to black and white lifestyles in the United States and raises the dilemma of how to endure it — through silence, as was the case with Du Bois, or exasperation, as was the case with Morrison? The collusion Baldwin points out, the mutual plotting, signifies that both the white insinuating the question — How does it feel to be a problem? — and the black who fails to respond with an indictment borne from years of suffering are evading the problem. Few blacks (Do any?) escape the awkwardness of such events that thrive on what is *not* said — that is, *How does it feel* to be other than the form of God? — even within the context of the church.

The similarities among Du Bois, Morrison, and Baldwin are striking regarding the problem, but the tradition they proffer is hardly "linear," essentialist, as if each writer were no more than a link in a chain — as if black consciousness were a monad. Nonetheless, Reed construes current appropriations of double-consciousness as attempts to affect a single Substance or Subjectivity, which, Reed alleges, serves "the vindicationist desire to establish the racial presence vis-à-vis a larger intellectual tradition." For Reed, the "most significant way that blacks figure into American intellectual life," that is, the "larger intellectual tradition," is through "their participation in the historically specific networks of shared presuppositions and concerns that shape the environing political discourse at any given moment...the Emerson/James/Du Bois nexus is instructive."[14]

It is to Du Bois's credit that he was sufficiently strong to hold his own in the "networks" of which Reed writes. Yet, while

Du Bois was a powerfully educated black American and as informed about the reigning intellectual paradigms of the day as most well-read scholars, white America limited his participation in "American intellectual life." As he put it near the end of his long life (1868–1963): "No American university (except Negro institutions in understandable self-defense) has ever recognized that I had any claim to scholarship."[15] Even today Du Bois is hardly as recognized as Ralph Waldo Emerson or William James in mainstream America, though Harvard's Du Bois Center is a notable exception. Why, then, undermine the alterity through which one sees that Du Bois "is against 'the winds and tides' of being"? Why not see him as "an interruption of essence...imposed with a good violence," to reiterate Levinas's sense of the "face"?[16] Du Bois's double-consciousness signifies the murmuring underside of American life rather than "a racially-framed version of a sentiment common among [his] contemporaries."[17]

Victor Anderson, the other critic of double-consciousness, construes Du Boisian "twoness" in terms of "ontological blackness." In deifying "the blackness that whiteness created," such an ontology "renders black life and experience a totality" and emphasizes "the heroic capacities of African Americans to transcend individuality and personality in the name of black communal survival."[18] With Reed, Anderson wants out of that *self*-veiled community as it cultivates rather than transcends the "binary dialectics of slavery and freedom."[19] For Anderson, double-consciousness perpetuates what blacks want to be free of, isolation, but again, is this the *only* way to read Du Bois: as a door that closes on "cultural fulfillment"?

Given its historical context, isn't it true that cultural fulfillment is the point of "Spiritual Strivings"? Du Bois argued that racism sabotaged blacks to such an extent that their efforts to pull themselves up by their bootstraps can be likened to trying to make bricks without straw. Still, Du Bois insisted that such injustice was no reason to fasten one's mind behind a plow. As he put it, "The end of [blacks' spiritual] striving [is] to be a co-worker in the kingdom of culture, *to escape both death and isolation*, to husband and use [their] best powers and...latent genius."[20] For the sake of that fulfilment, Du Bois, fluent in German and packing a degree from Berlin University, took on those banning blacks from the liberal arts. According to David Levering Lewis, then — and here he is similar to Reed — Du Bois uses double-consciousness very intentionally to demythologize the claim that the ex-slave is fit for little more than "home economics." "The construct was central to the fiction of Goethe and Chesnutt, two of [Du Bois's] favorite writers. Emerson, another favorite, had used the term 'double-consciousness' in 'The Transcendentalists.' "[21] Du Bois's appropriation of a common psychology, that is, double-consciousness, thus reflects his championing of the liberal arts, from which the Tuskegee Machine and its powerful Northern benefactors wanted to bar blacks.

In his *Dusk of Dawn*, the memoirs of a man in his seventies, Du Bois pointed out how the period from 1888, the year he graduated from Fisk, to the time of "Strivings," 1903, signified a certain narrowness: "I did not understand at all, nor had my history courses led me to understand, anything of current European intrigue, of the expansion of European power into Africa, of the Industrial Revolution built on the slave trade and now turning into Colonial Imperialism; of the fierce rivalry among white nations for controlling the profits from colonial raw material and labor — of all this I had no conception. I was blithely European and imperialist in outlook; democratic as democracy was conceived in America."[22] Although Du Bois points out his early subscription to a European outlook, his essay "The Conservation of Races," written in 1897, nonetheless foreshadows to a degree his radical conception of democracy, which led him to reject American citizenship in 1960. Surely the essay reveals the ontology in question, because Du Bois holds that "the history of the world is the history not of individuals but of groups, not of nations but of races, and he who ignores or seeks to override the race idea in human history ignores and overrides the central thought of all history."[23] The "race idea" — consider Hegel's *The Philosophy of History* — is a European concept. According to Du Bois, however, "great as is the physical unlikenesses of the various races . . . their likenesses are greater, and upon this rests the whole scientific doctrine of human brotherhood."[24] In "Conservation" and in "Strivings," then, Du Bois's commitment to human brotherhood opposed the master's limitation of one's possibilities based on race. Early on, Du Bois realized through his appropriation of double-consciousness, however Eurocentrically, that such limitation was a global problem: At the very dawning of the twentieth century, he asserted that its problem was the "color line" — "the relation of the darker to the lighter races of men in Asia and Africa, in America and the islands of the sea." In short, Du Bois's "twoness," linked as it is to what Victor Anderson calls "black communal survival," was a means to an end — *human* liberation — and *not* an end in itself.

Du Bois's waxing double-consciousness — as exemplified by *The Suppression of the Atlantic Slave Trade, The Negro, Black Reconstruction*, and the hindsight borne from his long life, that is, *Dusk of Dawn* and *The Autobiography of W. E. B. Du Bois* — reveals that the pertinence of double-consciousness is indeed progressive rather than parochial or resentfully ontological. Despite his chauvinism — and his later view that the black community had to become a separatist socialist world within a capitalist one — Du Bois's life is a spiritual movement toward the third person. Otherwise, he, so committed to economic and racial justice — and thus "cultural fulfillment" — for the world of color, would not be buried in Africa. Friend to Chairman Mao, hero to "Red" China, honored guest of Kwame Nkrumah, Du Bois, "the old man" as black American activists called him, was not bottled up in the "American-Negro thing." Rather, such double-consciousness was a *door* to what he was about in "Strivings" — human opportunity. Dogged strength can be appreciated as a commitment to human opportunity, to justice as well as peace, which burns through a nullifying Religion.

In the "Forethought" to *The Souls of Black Folk*, Du Bois remarks that he is "leaving the world of the white man," stepping "within the Veil, raising it that you may view faintly its deeper recesses, — the meaning of its religion, the passion of human sorrow, and the struggle of its greater souls." For me, Du Bois's stepping within the veil and "raising" it is — to make an allusion to Levinas — tantamount to the black face burning through the veil. In *Souls*, Du Bois destroys the stereotypes of black life with flammable faces — Josie, little Burghardt, Reverend Crummel — persons within his book who disclose "the struggle of its greater souls." "Raising," then, means more than lifting, for the veiled "destroy" their shroud with Du Bois's "good violence": Du Bois ruptures the circle of the Same in ways that bring to mind Emmanuel Levinas's critique of Sameness and its "Spirit."

According to Levinas, the Same and what burns through it, the Other, signify the foundation of socioeconomic structures, which humankind has infected with the inequalities of caste, race, and class. The lowest caste (or race or class), "the third person," has been in effect appropriated by the Same, as if the Other were nature rather than soul, becoming rather than being, chattel rather than human. For Levinas, that hateful appropriation of the Other has repressed the "Good," which is no faceless, untouchable, disembodied form or its modern actualization in the victors' Art and Religion. The Good is rather one's nonpaternalistic responsibility for the Other (the third person). For Levinas, that responsibility is discovered "in a tearing away of bread from the mouth that tastes it, to give it to the other" — a "coring out (*dénucléation*) of enjoyment, in which the nucleus of the ego is cored out."[25] The Good, therefore, is *not* the animus of "Spirit" and *its* "plastic activity" — the so-called "form of God" that actualizes itself through the negation integral to Hegel's epistemology.

Hegel negates Africa with his "Universal History," which grasps the import of time in terms of a "*Theodicaea* — a justification of the ways of God": "a harmonizing view...pressingly demanded ...in Universal History; and...attained only by recognizing the *positive* existence, in which that negative element is a subordinate, and vanquished nullity."[26] For Hegel, Africa was one such nullity. Because Africans enslaved other Africans — and because Hegel thought such enslavement summed up the meaning of African culture — we are to understand that Africans had no indigenous means to understand freedom. Hegel thus concludes "*slavery* to have been the occasion of the increase of human feeling among the Negroes."[27] As Hegel sees it, then, Africa's "Natural condition" is "one of absolute and thorough injustice — contravention of the Right and Just."[28] As the actuality of the Good, Europe nullifies Africa — the antithesis of being.

For Levinas, however, there is no such necessary nullification: "The Good as the infinite has no other, not because it would be the whole, but because it is Good and nothing escapes its goodness."[29] Not even the quaint and outlandish and heathen? Goodness thus desires the end of the master-slave dialectic so integral to the Religion's worldview. The emphasis on "Desire" is critical, for, according to Levinas, Desire differs from need. Need approaches the Other parasitically: Greedily, out of a drive analogous to hunger — privation (or what Sigmund Freud calls "aggression") — the master sadistically devours the slave. Desire, however, approaches the Other needlessly, seeks to communicate with the Other out of attraction to the future. This future depends on the cultivation of peace-with-justice.

Levinas's perspective calls to mind Du Bois's view that "the world of the white man," meaning for him western Europe and the United States, has been hostile to peace-with-justice on account of its parasitic hold on the Third World (especially Africa). For the

Du Bois of 1958, as I read him, Desire as commitment to peace, the future, meant *at least* that "the majority of the world's people who [were] unsheltered, with starvation and poverty," would "in reasonable time obtain a minimum supply of food, clothing and shelter, and the beginning of modern culture" only if "Western acquisitive society [paid] for it with less comfort, less luxury, and goods and privileges more equally divided."[30] Du Bois thought that the West refused "such sacrifice" (i.e., *dénucléation*) — and that for him was "the problem of the modern world."[31] Levinas makes a similar point. Du Bois's "modern world" is for Levinas the circle of the Same, which "does not recognize itself in its millennia of fratricidal, political, and bloody struggles, of imperialism, of human hatred and exploitation, up to our century of world wars, genocides, the Holocaust, and terrorism; of unemployment, the continuing poverty of the Third World."[32]

"Let us note again the difference between need and Desire: in need I can sink my teeth into the real and satisfy myself in assimilating the other; in Desire there is no sinking one's teeth into being, no satiety, but an uncharted future before me."[33] According to Levinas, then, Desire — goodness and justice — alone overcomes the problem of sameness writ large, which for the moment is the problem of what Du Bois has called the modern world, itself inextricable from the white man's religion. Levinasian Desire realizes that the Other's "face" transcends "the idea of the other in me":

> This *mode* [face] does not consist in figuring as a theme under my gaze, in spreading itself forth as a set of qualities forming an image. The face of the Other at each moment destroys and overflows the plastic image it leaves me, the idea existing to my own measure and to the measure of its *ideatum* — the adequate idea. It does not manifest itself by the invented "qualities," but ... *expresses itself.*[34]

"At each moment," the Other's face burns through "the plastic image," which signifies the veil that the Same fabricates. To put that another way, the face "signifies subjectivity or humanity, the *oneself* which repels the annexations by essence."[35] Burning through the veil, the shrouding activity of the white man's religion, the third person's face thus expresses what Du Bois calls "deeper recesses–the meaning of ... religion, the passion of human sorrow."[36] Or as Levinas puts it: The "Other comes ... outside, a separated — or holy — face. His [or her] exteriority, that is, his appeal to me, is his truth."[37]

Du Bois's truth is "a freedom struggling with its conqueror, re-fusing its reification and its objectification."[38] The epiphany wrecks the ontology, the form of God as "an avatar of the representation" of the Same, which demands capitulation to the master's salvation history.[39] In sum, the veil, the problem of the Same, involves these questions with which I am concerned in this book. Why is the master's form "God" while the slave's face is undesirable? Why do we *refuse* to see that it is impossible to understand the divine by way of "a look directed upon [God]"? Why won't we realize that "our possibility of welcoming [God in us] goes farther than the comprehension that thematizes and encompasses its object" through nullifying it?[40]

Africana Spirituality:
"Sometimes They Danced the Antelope"

Toni's Morrison's quote from her novel *Beloved* — "Sometimes they danced the antelope," referring to the Africans who survived the Middle Passage — directs us to possible answers to those questions. Morrison's antelope dance signifies a memory of a spirituality tied to agriculture and the womb, essential dimensions of a society that Francophone anthropologist Claude Meillassoux, author of *The Anthropology of Slavery: The Womb of Iron and Gold*, calls a "domestic non-slave society." Domestic non-slave society was agrarian; its dependence on the harvests made it imperative for its members to distribute subsistence crops evenly during the fallow periods and from harvest to harvest. The staples of the last harvest were thus stored so that the farmers would have the subsistence necessary to fuel the next season's planting. This value is based on "anteriority," that is, the ancestors, and hallows the bond between productive and nonproductive persons within the traditional society. Through this social value, which looks out for the very old and the very young, the unborn are promised a future: " 'We dig a well for tomorrow's thirst,' say the Maninka." The Mossi people express this bond among the living, the dead, and the unborn as follows: "Somebody looked after you until your teeth grew, look after him when his teeth fall out."[41]

The spirituality of domestic non-slave society is further observed in its absorption of aliens, casualties of war or products of "matrimonial or political strategies." Domestic non-slave societies widened "the passage of generations" by absorbing the progeny of "alien origin" until they were virtually indistinguishable from "the children of other families whose genealogical roots rarely go back further than five generations." The aliens' stigma was thus forgotten as they became producers whose children did not produce their ancestors' foreign heritage.[42]

Domestic non-slave society's tendency to "naturalize" aliens contrasts with the inhumanity of Africa's slave societies, in which, according to Meillassoux, the victims of the patrilineal societies of the African Savannah were "living livestock, without any of the pretenses resorted to in avuncular societies. [These] slaves had no rights."[43] While, then, the survivors of the Middle Passage had been victims of the African slave trade, which preyed on domestic non-slave society, the first generation rejected their new owners' Religion in favor of their humane traditions, their Africana spirituality. As a mode of Africana spirituality, Morrison's antelope dance signifies a particular "form" of consciousness, that is, memory, which empowers one to explore traces of historic connections between Africans and African Americans. In addition, the dance signifies Lewis Gordon's definition of Africana thought: the focus on "theoretical questions raised by struggles over ideas in African cultures and their hybrid and creolized forms in Europe, North America, Central and South America, and the Caribbean."[44] As a trace of domestic non-slave society, as a hybrid form of African culture, Morrison's antelope dance thus brings to mind the memory of the ancestors' "relationship with the sun and the earth, the stars and seasons, animals and plants, iron and the techniques of producing agricultural tools, and clothing and ornaments" — the principle of fecundity.[45] The antelope dance burns through Hegel's notion of Absolute Spirit. The ancestors are not nullifiable as "the natural man in his completely wild and untamed state."[46] The dance, theoretically a mode of African peasant or African slave spirituality, was itself freedom when compared to the Religion; for any religion that nullifies a people's self-apprehension is — as Countee Cullen suggests — too high priced. "Converts" to the Religion are hardly saved when their nullification is tantamount to their freedom.

The prohibitiveness of such freedom accounts for why African scholar V. Y. Mudimbe asks, "From the margins of Christianity or, more exactly, *from the margins of a Western history that institutionalized Christianity*, how can one not think that what is going on here is a simple exegesis of a well-localized and tautological tradition that seems incapable of imagining the very possibility of its exteriority, namely, that, in its margins, other historical traditions can also be credible, meaningful, respectable, and sustained by relatively well-delineated historicities"?[47] His question is critical, for if the form of the master is "God," then we really would be "facing something like a firmly closed circle": Why is the master's form God? *Because of this firmly closed circle*. To put that another way, Europeans' and (Euro-) Americans' biblical hermeneutics are steeped in their cultural traditions. Given their languages, philosophies, and icons, through which Christianity has persisted in time, one can truthfully say that Christian spirituality has been essentially European and Euro-American spirituality. Is there now no time for Africana spirituality?

"Time . . . Violent with the Mysterious Love of God"

"The mysterious love of God," the theme from James Baldwin's novel *Go Tell It on the Mountain*, responds to that question of whether there is time for Africana spirituality. In the novel, Baldwin's protagonist, John Grimes (the representation of Baldwin himself), succumbs to the angst of his black church experience and so begins to question the connection between Christianization and chattelization:

> Fury and anguish filled [John Grimes], unbearable, unanswerable; his mind was stretched to breaking. For it was time that filled his mind, time that was violent with the mysterious love of God. And his mind could not contain the terrible stretch of time that united twelve men fishing by the shores of Galilee, and black men weeping on their knees tonight, and he, a witness. . . . There was an awful silence at the bottom of John's mind, a dreadful weight, a dreadful speculation. And not even speculation, but a deep, deep turning, as of something huge, black, shapeless, for ages dead on the ocean floor, that now felt its rest disturbed by a faint, far wind, which bid it: 'Arise.' And this weight began to move at the bottom of John's mind, in a silence like the silence of the void before creation, and he began to feel a terror he had never felt before.[48]

Baldwin's emphasis on time, through which the Africans' descendants became American Christians, suggests that God's love burdens African American Christians more than it does the Protestant settlers' descendants sure that God is in their image. For Baldwin, their Religion is responsible for the black church, which is for Baldwin a slave institution to be overcome by a spirituality more original than the form of God. For something ageless — "like the silence of the void before creation" — was at work in that church's African-like charisma. The blacks "weeping on their knees" within the veil love Jesus' God, the mysterious source of love, despite the *aporia* that rocks that church hewn out of slavery.

That double-consciousness of God's love and human suffering entails the tension between what Levinas calls the "thought of the infinite" and the "thought of the finite."[49] "Thought of the finite" signifies fury and anguish, the aforementioned *aporia*, brought on by the Protestant Religion that has forced the weeping blacks to their knees. "Thought of the infinite" — "which is older than thought of the finite" and "the very diachrony of time" — signifies the mysterious love that transcends the finite Religion. Diachrony, a mode of transcendence, refers to the past and the future, the dead and the unborn. The links between them are the veiled persons themselves, who are in between yesterday and tomorrow. "Weeping on their knees *tonight*," they are suspended in "the terrible stretch of *time*," the diachrony, "that united [them to] twelve men fishing by the shores of Galilee." On the basis of that connection, which "his mind could not contain," Baldwin's John senses the hugeness of the past — an "immemorial" more enormous than the white man's religion. John's fury and anguish, moreover, suggests tacitly that the mysterious love of God unfurls from the future — is *more* elastic than the American church that "civilizes," as in nullifies, with millenarian pretense. "For it was *time* that filled his mind, *time* that was violent *with the mysterious love of God*." The future, God's own time, is thus vaster than the past, and this will instill great hope in John.

I believe "the terrible stretch of time" also signifies a memory that is more immediate than that about twelve fishermen. This memory is what terrifies John, for it signifies the Middle Passage: "something huge, black, shapeless, for ages dead on the ocean floor." For the sake of the *future* of its casualties, Baldwin's memory of the Middle Passage thus signifies the *present*-ness of the past in the "deepest thought, which carries all thought" — thought as memory and hope.[50] "Being-that-is-no-longer" and "Being-that-is-not-yet" are thus bridged, "present through the force of remembrance and expectation."[51]

For the sake of the dead and the unborn (and the readers' sakes too), Baldwin's witness to blacks weeping on their knees — who so dutifully recite the Third Article, "I believe in the Holy Spirit, the Lord and giver of life" — thus raises a critical question: Whose "Spirit" withstands the terrible perception of "something huge, black, shapeless, for ages dead on the ocean floor"? The apotheosis, the synchrony, of the Same — the thought of the finite: "the identifying of death with nothingness [so as to legitimize] the death of the other in murder"?[52] Or is the Spirit the infinite signified in one's spirit by the responsible ethic — "Thou shall not kill"? The pliant memory of the Passage, the *time* involved in one's present *aporia*, thus surfaces undesirable faces until they burn through the thought of the finite — the Religion in question. Baldwin thus "realizes impossibility: memory, after the event, assumes the passivity of the past and masters it. Memory as an inversion of historical time is the essence of interiority [i.e., spirituality]."[53] As an inversion of historical time, memory is futuristic, for only the future can stretch backward through the present for the sake of the dead. As spirituality, that is, interiority, this inversion therefore assumes responsibility for the nullified — the casualties of the Middle Passage. Their salty bones — "for ages dead on the ocean floor" — are murmuring artifacts in one's spirituality.

One realizes through this spirituality that "at the centre of Christian theology stands the eternal history which the triune God experiences in himself. Every narrative needs *time*. For the narrative in which [we] praise the triune God [we] need ... time too."[54] Surely the future — the resurrection of the dead — would liberate the alterity of the past, which is much more than what the universal historian has *said*, his abridged narrative. So one's memory of the Middle Passage "is more appropriate for the eternal divine present than the abstractions in which time is dissolved."[55] One, then, should render attempts to nullify the memory of the slave ships and non-slave domestic societies suspect if the God whom troubled Christians hope unceasingly to praise is as much a God of the dead as of the living.

Given the hegemony of Euro-American hermeneutics, can the claim that Christ dies for *us* withstand such "fury and anguish" — the diachrony involved in veiled generations weeping on their knees? As William Jones put it, "The interval between Cross and

Resurrection was by no means a millennium."[56] Can one truly
hold that the resurrection from the dead includes blacks weeping
on their knees, blacks who represent what Jones calls "unrelieved
suffering" or "transgenerational suffering"?[57] Time — the making good of an "apocatastatic" promise — will tell. In short, the
theme "the mysterious love of God" is concerned with theodicy:
Why, indeed, is the master's form God while the slave's face is undesirable — anchored to the Atlantic's watery depths? And why,
indeed, is God content with "the comprehension that thematizes
and encompasses its object"?[58]

As the unity of a hermeneutics of suspicion and a marginalized
body, *Dogged Strength within the Veil: Africana Spirituality and
the Mysterious Love of God* offers the *faces* of black essayists and
novelists, principally Du Bois, Morrison, and Baldwin. Through
these faces and their Africana spirituality, I suffer what Baldwin
has called "a deep, deep turning, as of something huge, black,
shapeless, for ages dead on the ocean floor" — the Middle Passage. This suffering enables me to contextualize Levinas's view that
"in the totality of the historiographer [i.e., the universal historian]
the death of the Other is an *end*, the point at which the separated
being is cast into the totality, and at which, consequently, *dying*
can be passed through and past, the point from which the separated being will continue by virtue of the heritage his existence
had amassed."[59] As a Christianized progeny of the nullified, then,
I should be grateful for my ancestors' absorption into the state, the
costliness of that absorption notwithstanding. Yet my spirituality
resists the totalization that renders my *African* heritage "nothing
but past." My spirituality thus refuses to allow my ancestors "to
be transformed into a pure loss figuring in an alien accounting
system."[60] In touch with them, I understand Levinas's assertion
that the

> death agony is precisely in this impossibility of ceasing, in the
> ambiguity of a time that has run out and of a mysterious time
> that yet remains; death is consequently not reducible to the
> end of a being. What "still remains" is totally different from
> the future that one welcomes, that one projects forth and in
> a certain measure draws from oneself. For a being to whom
> everything happens in conformity with projects, death is an
> absolute event, absolutely a posteriori, open to no power,
> not even negation. Dying is agony because in dying a being
> does not come to an end while coming to an end; he has no

> more time, that is, can no longer wend his way anywhere, but thus he goes where one cannot go, suffocates — how much longer ... [61]

How *much* longer? I take that to mean that those who fail to suffer their dead — to suffocate (as in crouch) *with* them as Toni Morrison does magically in *Beloved* and James Baldwin in *Go Tell It on the Mountain* and W. E. B. Du Bois in *Black Reconstruction* — are not justice- and future-oriented, are not hopeful. These writers remind us that we come through the dead: forgetfulness of their struggles dehumanizes us and cultivates a callousness toward time and the possibilities it affords us. Those who "forget" that the "death agony is precisely in this impossibility of ceasing" are hostile to those, our grandsons and granddaughters, who will tread above us. Through Du Bois, Morrison, Baldwin, the Africana spirit — an African and an American spirit — encounters the faces below and seeks their counterparts in Africa and America today. Moved by the mysterious love of God, ineffably elastic, I will thus explore Africana spirituality as a dogged strength attentive to who is "down there," who is here, and who is to come. In short, this book is about the inner strength — the insight into one's hopes and one's oppression — that empowers one to burn through a nullifying double standard for the dead, the living, and the unborn.

Part Two

Dogged Strength within the Veil

Double-Consciousness and the Shrouding Activity of the White Man's Religion

Chapter 3

"Nobody Knows
the Trouble I've Seen"

Du Bois's Inner Strength

When, struck with a sudden poverty, the United States refused to fulfill its promises of land to the freedman, a brigadier-general went down to the Sea Islands to carry the news. An old woman on the outskirts of the throng began singing this song; all the mass joined with her, swaying. And the soldier wept. — W. E. B. DU BOIS[1]

In *Dusk of Dawn,* Du Bois recounts his introduction to the "scientific race dogma" his professors taught while he was a student at Harvard (1888–1891). Harvard professors taught evolution and the survival of the fittest, a perspective that was pervasive throughout the campus — "continually stressed in the community and in classes." Whites asserted that they were calculably superior to nonwhite people, as attested, for instance, by the "physical development of the Negro." Du Bois recalls being in a museum in which he studied a display: "a series of skeletons arranged from a little monkey to a tall well-developed white man, with a Negro barely outranking a chimpanzee." Such science took subtler forms in his classes that emphasized "brain weight and brain capacity, and at last...the 'cephalic index.' "[2]

On the Negro

Years later when the nation crowded blacks into Jim Crow cars, threatened them with the lynch rope, and was hostile to his scholarship, Du Bois took on the fittest as he faced what he called "that nameless prejudice...that personal disrespect and mockery, the ridicule and systematic humiliation, the distortion of fact and wanton license of fancy, the cynical ignoring of the better and bois-terous welcoming of the worst, the all-pervading desire to inculcate disdain for everything black from Toussaint to the devil."[3] While he did not wish to "Africanize" America, for he thought "America has too much to teach the world and Africa," Du Bois "would not bleach his Negro soul in a flood of white Americanism."[4] Believing that "Negro blood has a message for the world," he would not, then, nullify his black African ancestors, who made it impossible for him to "pass" (for white). "I felt myself African by 'race,' " Du Bois writes in *Dusk of Dawn,* "and by that token was African and an integral member of the group of dark Americans who were called Negroes."[5] Du Bois, the progeny of slaves and slave holders, used his ancestry — his mother's line descended from an African woman — to disprove racist, bourgeois "science." Du Bois thus sought to take on those who thought black blood would weaken "civilization." He found nothing "more fascinating than the ques-tion of the various types of mankind and their intermixture" and held that such blending was itself the key to the "whole question of heredity and human gift."[6] Du Bois argues that "we have been afraid in America that scientific study in this direction might lead to conclusions with which we were loath to agree; and this fear was in reality because the economic foundation of the modern world was based on the recognition and preservation of so-called racial distinctions."[7]

Du Bois published *The Negro* in 1915 to expose further the hatefulness that funded racist logic. *The Negro* argues that the black body, Africa's metonym, signifies no inferior hominid but "a sheer fight for physical survival comparable with that in no other great continent."[8] Du Bois, then, held that the Bantu's round-houses do not signify an abundance of black blood while the French's cathedrals signify the absolute lack of it. Neither cathe-drals nor thatched huts signify blood, that is, race, but rather the opportunities that environments afford human innovation. As Jared Diamond argues in his Pulitzer Prize-winning *Guns, Germs, and Steel,* "history followed different courses for different peoples because of differences among people's environments, not because of biological differences among people themselves."[9]

The Negro argues, moreover, that there is no pure, that is, un-mixed, human type. According to Du Bois, humankind evolved out of southern Asia and began to differentiate in migrating to southern, eastern, and northern Asia. Du Bois calls those who migrated to the south and into Africa the "primitive Negro," who was "long-headed" and kinky haired and akin today to pygmies of Central Africa and the Khoisan of southern Africa.[10] Du Bois writes that the initial migration to Africa was followed thousands of years later by another wave of "Asiatic people, Negroid in many characteristics, but lighter and straighter haired than the primitive Negroes." For Du Bois, those people are the ancestors of those living on "the shores of the Mediterranean in Europe, Asia, and Africa."[11] In Africa, that wave of Afro-Asiatics meshed with the "primitive Negroid stock" issuing over time into the ancient Egyptians and modern Negroid races of Africa. For Du Bois, then, the history of migrations into Africa made it home to "every degree of development in Negroid stocks."[12] What is more, Du Bois argues that all of the world's people stem from Asia's primal miscegenation: Early Europe and Asia were as mixed as Africa; but whereas the "mulattos," as Du Bois called them, were whitened by the environment in Asia and Europe, they were blackened in Africa. In short, neither whites nor blacks are pure types — polar entities between which other "races" line up. "No such absolute type ever existed on either side. Both were slowly differentiated from a common ancestry and continually remingled their blood."[13]

Current scholarship deems it probable that "anatomically modern humans" (*homo sapiens sapiens*) populated the earth from Africa rather than Asia. Yet current scholarship agrees with Du Bois that "European" and "African" signify the diversity of a single, blended human type. So-called racial differences, then, are owed to diverse inhabitation patterns and the environmental pressures basic to them. "The major stereotypes, all based on skin color, hair color and form, and facial traits, reflect superficial differences that are not confirmed by deeper analysis with more reliable genetic traits and whose origin dates from recent evolution mostly under the effect of climate and perhaps sexual selection."[14]

For Du Bois, black Africans have *never* been biologically inferior human types: "Primitive life among them is, after all, as bare and cruel as among primitive Germans or Chinese, but it is not more so, and the more we study the Negro the more we realize that we are dealing with a normal human stock which under reasonable conditions has developed and will develop in the same lines as other[s]."[15] "Why is it, then," asks Du Bois, "that so much of misinformation and contempt is widespread concerning Africa and its people, not simply among the unthinking mass, but among men of education and knowledge?"[16] The answer for Du Bois was the Middle Passage, which, according to him, was the work of "the most ruthless class of...mercantile exploiters." Civilization granted them a "large liberty, if not a free hand, and protected" them through "a concerted attempt to deify white men."[17] Du Bois goes on to observe that the Middle Passage occurred in "the day of the greatest expansion of two of the world's most pretentious religions and of the beginnings of the modern organization of industry." As Europe experienced its Enlightenment and America its "free" nationhood, "slavery spread more human misery, inculcated more disrespect for and neglect of humanity, a greater callousness to suffering, and more petty, cruel, human hatred than can well be calculated. We may excuse and palliate it," writes Du Bois, "and write history so as to let men forget it; it remains the most inexcusable and despicable blot on human history."[18]

One Ever Feels This Twoness

In 1999 I led a student group to Ghana to pay respects to the author of *The Negro*. Indeed, the students had become interested in Ghana because of their awareness of African Americans' historic, high-priced conversion. We were "One three centuries removed / From the scenes [our] fathers loved," as the poet Countee Cullen put it in his poem "Heritage," but two monuments brought Ghana close to home (to double-consciousness): the fortress where the slaves were held, Elmina, built by the Portuguese in the late fifteenth century, and the Du Bois Center in Accra, where Du Bois is now buried. In Ghana one encounters "the door of no return," the portal of the slave castles from which the enslaved were taken from Africa. And there one may stand above the bones of W. E. B. Du Bois.

During our sojourn in Ghana, Du Bois's double-consciousness took on new meaning. I was given yet another way to ponder being American and "Negro." During one of the seminar sessions that our host, African theologian Mercy Oduyoye, set up for us, the discussion turned to the white Jesus (the "form of God"). My students wanted to know why he was pictured in all of the churches we visited. Many of the Ghanians argued that the facial type of the icon was not important; what it signified, God, was the essential thing. Surely one can argue that the icon really does not matter. Mercy Oduyoye pointed out something along the lines of

"We know Jesus didn't come from here, so it's okay," but she also acknowledged the students' concerns: Doesn't one acquiesce in the colonial continuum in hanging that symbol no African had produced? What happened to the struggle to divest the faith of its ties to colonialism? What about the belief of African theologian Kä Mana that the African church must be the heart of a new society in a new, about-to-be-born Africa?[19] Wouldn't that mean that the church itself would have to nurture a faithful spirituality, fecundly rooted in African cultures, and thus step up to the task of evangelizing the Continent?[20]

As the students began to press the issue about the "form of God," one of the members of the Ghanian community called us *oburoni*, meaning whites. We were called whites by virtue of our "Americanness." We had been enslaved by the white man, bore his name, and were, figuratively and in most cases literally, flesh of his flesh. The word *oburoni*, however, also reminded us of the historic role Ghanians played in our enslavement. The Asante elite fed the Middle Passage and had in fact a long history of enslaving other "Negroes." The Asante carved the city of Kumase, the heart and soul of the Asante people, out of the rain forests with "unfree labor." As Ivor Wilkes put it in his *Forest of Gold:* "The historical record . . . shows that unfree labor was being drawn into the forestlands from both north and south in the very period in which — if we have interpreted Asante traditions clearly — forest clearances were underway. . . . The availability of labor was a necessary precondition of those clearances and therefore of the creation of the agrarian order."[21] One of the students pointed out through an impassioned appeal to *"Exterminate All the Brutes"* — a book by Sven Lindqvist about how Europeans also made the Africans *oburoni* — that black Africa bears the white man's image too.

The label *oburoni* would not undermine why we had come to Ghana. We had come instructed by Du Bois's double-consciousness — so we are *oburoni* in part — and with a memory of how most Africans had become Christians. We had come bearing Du Bois's legacy — "to build . . . on decency of hand and heart."[22] We had come to Ghana with something to offer discussions on Christology in Africa. The students were merely attempting to raise the suspicion that the contested icon signifies Hegel's notion of "the identity of the Subject and God . . . introduced into the World *when the fulness of Time was come:* the . . . recognition of God in his true essence . . . manifested to man *in the Christian Religion.*"[23]

Levinas has found that "memory...assumes the passivity of the past and masters it...as an inversion of historical time," and that this inversion is "the essence of interiority [i.e., spirituality]."[24] Our spirituality was such that we thought of ourselves partly as "reincarnations" of those who had passed through the door of no return. "We survived," said one of the students (the one who made the reference to *"Exterminate All the Brutes"*). She assumed the passivity of yesterday and mastered it with an appropriate double-consciousness. We discovered that we are as "Negro" as the Twi-speaking Ghanians, and that *oburoni,* inextricable from the Middle Passage, take many forms.

At bottom, Du Bois's inner strength empowered us to resist vestiges of enslavement to the form of God and overcome all put-downs that would split us in two and deter us from the goal — human opportunity for all. Surely Du Bois's inner strength has taught me to focus on the real issue, which Du Bois expressed admirably in his essay "Of Our Spiritual Strivings": "that vaster ideal that swims before the Negro people, the ideal of human brotherhood, gained through the unifying ideal of Race; the ideal of fostering and developing the traits and talents of the Negro, not in opposition to or contempt for other races."[25]

Our Spiritual Strivings Revisited

After the experiences in Ghana, after visiting Du Bois's grave, I reread a speech he gave in China in 1959 when the Chinese made Du Bois's birthday a national holiday. He pleaded for unity between China and Africa. He also pleaded for Africa and the Diaspora — "Africa in Africa and all your children's children overseas" — to realize the depth of their miseducation and the abuse that had fostered it: "You have been told and the telling so beaten into you by rods and whips, that you believe it yourselves, that... mankind can rise only by walking on men; by cheating them and killing them; that only on a doormat of the despised and dying, the dead and rotten, can a British aristocracy, or a French cultural elite or an American millionaire be nurtured and grown. This is a lie."[26] For Du Bois, such mendacity is "an ancient lie spread by church and state, spread by priest and historian, and believed in by fools and cowards, as well as by the downtrodden and the children of despair."[27] I must agree: It is a lie, and that it is, is God's truth (in third-person hermeneutics at any rate). This truth wells up from within the veil, from Du Bois's claim that he speaks to African people from China — to the third person from the context of "thirdness" — with neither authority nor money, but from his own dogged strength: "One thing alone I own and that is my own soul. Ownership of that I have even while in my own country for near a century I have been nothing but a 'nigger.' On this basis and this alone I dare speak, I dare advise."[28]

His bitterness — "I have been nothing but a 'nigger' " — compellingly directs us to ask again: "How does it feel to be a problem?" How does it feel to be black in the United States of America — to have to see oneself through "the other world"? The question underlies Du Bois's observation that blacks have "no true self-consciousness." For self-consciousness, as in black consciousness, must have constantly measured itself against a racist ideal, the form of God, which sabotages black self-esteem. And that, for Du Bois, is "a peculiar sensation, this double-consciousness, this sense of always looking at one's self through the eyes of others, of measuring one's soul by the tape of a world that looks on in amused contempt and pity." Dogged strength within the veil, the black person's will to be more than the white world's negative image, is a wonder and a pain.

The wonder of it for Du Bois was his ability to resist and expose the hatefulness that would tear apart his spirit — through which he realized that there was nothing, after all, wrong with *him*. He writes in *Darkwater* that his clairvoyance made him acutely aware of the meanness of those who had deprived him of an inner life free from racist projection. He writes, "Not as a foreigner do I come, for I am native, not foreign, bone of their thought and flesh of their language."[29] As an expert on the dysfunction of white folks, he unveils "the working of their entrails...their thoughts." Despite the fact that they call him "misbirth!" he sees them "ever stripped, — ugly, human."[30] Yet his insight caused him tremendous pain. Several events come to mind.

The first is the lynching of Sam Hose in 1899, which occurred just outside Atlanta where Du Bois was a professor of economics and history at Atlanta University. A lynch mob dismembered and barbecued Hose and fought for pieces of his flesh. The aggression depressed Du Bois. Informed that Hose's barbecued knuckles were on view in a white storeowner's window not far from where Du Bois taught at Atlanta University, Du Bois found himself unable to work, nauseated because a part of Hose's body had become a curio item, and a warning. Du Bois realized that he "could not be a calm, cool, and detached scientist while Negroes were lynched, murdered, and starved."[31] The Sam Hose event thus pushed Du Bois toward becoming a human rights activist.

The second event, the death of Du Bois's two-year-old son, Burghardt, who died from the "nasopharyngeal diphtheria" that Du Bois attributed to the "city's careless sewage," occurred not long after the Sam Hose horror. None of the few black doctors was available when the boy's condition threatened his life. In his pain, Du Bois remarked, "Well sped, my boy, before the world had dubbed your ambition insolence, had held your ideas unattainable, and taught you how to cringe and bow. Better far this nameless void that stops my life than a sea of sorrows for you."[32] Even with his sense that death had freed his son from racist limitations, Du Bois remained committed to burning through the veil. In the wake of little Burghardt's death, Du Bois set to work "for fresh young souls who have not known the night and waken to the morning; a morning when men ask of the workman, not 'Is he white?' but 'Can he work?' When men ask artists, not 'Are they black?' but 'Do they know?'"[33]

In addition to those two events, a powerful Northern oligarchy compounded Du Bois's stress. Its inner circle — Robert Ogden, William Baldwin, George Foster Peabody, John D. Rockefeller — lauded and financed Tuskegee and Hampton under the auspices of the Southern Education Board (SEB) and the General Education Board (GEB). According to Du Bois, those organizations helped to institutionalize the subservience of blacks as they held that to teach black children as if they were on par with white ones would defy reason. Practicality alone was the cure for such enthusiasm: Blacks were to learn to celebrate prejudice borne of necessity — "the place of Negroes must be that of a humble, patient, hard-working group of laborers, whose ultimate destiny would be determined by their white employers."[34] White children alone were to prepare to become philosophers and physicians, and the blacks were to receive "elementary instruction, and more especially...training in farming and industry, calculated to make the mass of Negroes laborers contented with their lot and cheap."[35] Given his embodiment of the education they thought blacks incapable of mastering, the SEB and the GEB viewed Du Bois as a dangerous figure. They used their wealth and political clout to marginalize him. Still, Du Bois continued, doggedly, to fight them for the sake of human opportunity.

The beacon of Du Bois's dogged strength remains his *Black Reconstruction*. As he probes the recesses of the veil in that massive study, he is at points theologically profound. Especially moving is Du Bois's conclusion of the chapter in *Black Reconstruction* entitled "The Coming of the Lord":

> Suppose on some gray day, as you plod down Wall Street, you should see God sitting on the Treasury steps, in His Glory, with the thunders curved about him? Suppose on Michigan Avenue, between the lakes and hill of stone, and in the midst of hastening automobiles and jostling crowds, suddenly you see living and walking toward you, the Christ, with sorrow and sunshine in his face? Foolish talk all of this, you say, of course; and that is because no American now believes in his religion. Its facts are mere symbolism, its revelation vague generalities; its ethics a matter of carefully balanced gain. But to most of the four million black folk emancipated by civil war, God was real. They knew Him. They had met Him personally in many a wild orgy of religious frenzy, or in the black stillness of the night. His plan for them was clear; they were to suffer and be degraded, and then afterwards by Divine edict, raised to [humanity] and power; and so on January 1, 1863, He made them free.[36]

According to Du Bois, 1863 was the "Apocalypse" for the mass of black folk. "The magnificent trumpet tones of Hebrew Scripture, transmuted and oddly changed, became a strange new gospel. All that was Beauty, all that was Love, all that was Truth, stood on the top of these mad mornings and sang with the stars. A great human sob shrieked in the wind, and tossed its tears upon the sea, — free, free, free."[37]

The state, however, began to abuse that freedom in 1865 with the historic betrayal of the ex-slaves in South Carolina. Du Bois writes of the abolitionist Union officer General Howard, who informed the Charleston blacks that the land given to them during the course of the war as the Union's sign of good faith was to be returned to their former masters. "General Howard was called upon to address them, and to cover his own confusion and sympathy he asked them to sing. Immediately an old woman on the outskirts of the meeting began 'Nobody Knows the Trouble I've Seen.' Howard wept."[38] He wept because he began to discover in himself a heightened vulnerability to, and an intensified responsibility for, the third person.

Du Bois writes of another betrayal of the ex-slaves. According to Du Bois, "The revolution of 1876 was, in fine, a victory for which the South has every right to hang its head. After enslaving the Negro for two and one-half centuries, it turned on his emancipation to beat a beaten man, to trade in slaves, and to kill the defenseless; to break the spirit of the [blacks]...and humiliate [them] into hopelessness; to establish a new dictatorship of property in the South through the color line. It was a triumph of men who in their effort to replace equality with caste and to build inordinate wealth on a foundation of abject poverty have succeeded in killing democracy, art and religion."[39] Du Bois writes of that betrayal: "God wept; but that mattered little to an unbelieving age; what mattered most was that the world wept and is still weeping and blind with tears and blood."[40]

Nobody knows the trouble I've seen; / Nobody knows but Jesus: While Du Bois is cynical about American Christianity because of its captivity to the form of God, he conveys third persons' hope that the Spirit of Christ burns through the veil in solidarity with them. Here Du Bois is neither cynical nor derisively agnostic, but a dedicated scribe in service to those who lived in anticipation of the Son of Man *and* in the spirit of the Man of Sorrows. Through Du Bois we remember "earnest and bewildered...faces...ground in the mud by their three centuries of degradation and who now staggered forward blindly in blood and tears amid petty division, hate and hurt, and surrounded by every disaster of war and industrial upheaval."[41]

Chapter 4

American Africanism

Toni Morrison's Insight into the Form of God

My project is an effort to avert the critical gaze from the racial object to the racial subject; from the described and imagined to the describers and imaginers; from the serving to the served. — TONI MORRISON[1]

In *Playing in the Dark: Whiteness and the Literary Imagination*, Toni Morrison writes, "American means white, and Africanist people struggle to make the term applicable to themselves with ethnicity and hyphen after hyphen after hyphen."[2] She recasts Du Bois's dilemma — "How does it feel to be a problem?" — as follows: "What happens to the writerly imagination of a black author who is at some level *always* conscious of representing one's own race to, or in spite of, a race of readers" dreaming that they are "universal or race-free"?[3]

An Abusive Somnolence: American Africanism

One thing that happens is that the black author, in this case Morrison, plunges further back than the Reconstruction to discover the roots of those dreaming that they are universal. She takes us back to the English who colonized North America to forge a New World. The colonists Americanized their best traditions — their jurisprudence, their literary traditions, their churches — and their Old World prejudice against blacks. According to historian Winthrop Jordan, the English "frequently described the Africans as 'brutish' or 'bestial' or 'beastly,'" as extensions of exotic species —

45

lions, hyaenas, and so forth. "In making this instinctive analogy, Englishmen unwittingly demonstrated how powerfully the
African's different culture — for Englishmen, his 'savagery' — op-
erated to make Negroes seem to Englishmen a radically different
kind of men."[4] The colonists, themselves Anglo-Saxons, brought
such views with them to the New World. They appropriated the
"beastly" Africans as "surrogate selves" who assuaged white anx-
ieties in an unknown territory. The black body symbolized both
whites' angst in a menacing territory and their domination of nature. According to Morrison, the whites thus used their slaves, their
"surrogate selves," to contemplate freedom "in terms other than
the abstractions of human potential and the rights of man."[5] Morrison calls this parasitical freedom — this need "to allay internal
fears and to rationalize external exploitation" at the expense of
blacks — "American Africanism": the "views, assumptions, read-
ings, and misreadings that accompany Eurocentric learning about
[African] people."[6] Given the legacy of American Africanism, Morrison must manage two warring ideals, for "living in a nation of
people who *decided* that their world view would combine agendas for individual freedom *and* mechanisms for devastating racial
oppression presents a singular landscape for a writer."[7] Yet she refuses to be torn asunder. Morrison expresses herself despite the
ontology whose "somnambulist's tread is insufficient to separate
from the center of the world."[8] To show how this is so, I return to
her scorching story, *Beloved*.

"Oh but When They Danced" within the Veil

Having created *Beloved* as if she had been born with a caul, Morrison places the reader in that watershed time, the Civil War and
Reconstruction, which Du Bois records for posterity in "Of Our
Spiritual Strivings." He writes of an era that was "merely a prolon-
gation of the vain search for freedom, the boon that seemed ever
barely to elude [blacks'] grasp, — like a tantalizing will-o'-the-wisp,
maddening and misleading the headless host. The holocaust of war,
the terrors of the Ku Klux Klan, the lies of carpetbaggers, the dis-
organization of industry, and the contradictory advice of friends
and foes, left the bewildered serf no new watchword beyond the
old cry for freedom."[9] *Beloved* surfaces the murmuring faces that
had been submerged and carries the memory of the colonial past
and its African background.

Beloved focuses on an ex-slave woman, Sethe, and her daughters, Denver and Beloved. In 1855 Sethe escaped the slave state of Kentucky, but the Fugitive Slave Act of 1850 empowered her "owner," whom she called "schoolteacher," to come after her and her highly prized children. Rather than surrender her children to him, she acts to put them beyond the reach of slavery. Sethe "collected every bit of life she had made, all the parts of her that were precious and fine and beautiful" — two boys and two girls — "and carried, pushed, dragged them through the veil, out, away, over there where no one could hurt them. Over there. Outside this place, where they would be safe."[10] Sethe runs to a shed where she intends to liberate all her children, but she only has time to "free" Beloved, her "crawling-already?" daughter of nine months: Sethe slits her baby's throat to free her from slavery. Unable to sleep the sleep of death, Beloved emerges eighteen years later from a stream behind the woods. For me, the stream symbolizes the Atlantic Ocean, the Middle Passage, and thus the link between Africans and African Americans. Whether my conjecture is true, the novel has many implications for Africana thought.

Sethe remembers that when she, pregnant with Denver, escaped from Kentucky, she fell exhausted to the earth. Her unborn child, whom she called "the little antelope," "rammed her with horns and pawed the ground of her womb with impatient hooves." "And why she thought of an antelope Sethe could not imagine since she had never seen one."[11] She answers her question by connecting her fawn to her African-born mother and the other Africans on the large plantation in the deep South where Sethe was born. Sethe fondly remembers the slave culture in which she had been raised. "Oh but when they sang," writes Morrison, rendering Sethe's memory. "And oh but when they danced and sometimes they danced the antelope. The men as well as the ma'ams, one of whom was certainly [Sethe's mother]. They shifted shapes and became something other. *Some unchained, demanding other* whose feet knew [Sethe's] pulse better than she did. Just like this one in her stomach."[12]

The fact that Sethe's "little antelope" occasions the memory of that male and female dance suggests that a Bambara spirituality is a part of her heritage. The Bambara are West Africans, some of whom were abducted in the transatlantic trade. Their antelope mask — three sculpted figures, the female, the male, and the fawn — symbolizes fecundity. According to one source: "The female antelope, the Earth, whose high, upright and rigid horns

symbolize the growing of the seeds in the damp soil, is also the
Mother of [humankind], as represented by the fawn she bears on
her back. Above the fawn, the male...with its full flowing mane
is suggestive of the sun whose warmth fertilizes the earth. The
chevron pattern round his neck symbolizes...the zig-zag course
followed by the sun."[13] More is at stake, then, than singing and
dancing. Morrison plunges back further than American Africanism
and sees in the haze a wholesome orientation to life.

Far from being the irrational savages Hegel dreamed that they
were, the Bambara have an elaborate cosmology. Dominique Zahan points out in his *La dialectique du verbe chez les Bambara*
(*The Bambara's Dialectic of the Verbe*) that the Bambara's highest aspiration is knowledge of the diffused manifestations of the
Creator, Bemba. Whether one speaks truth or falsehood, or sows
harmony or discord, attests to whether one circulates theistic
values that the Bambara summarize as Bemba's Word.

Bemba's diversity is personified in the three primordial beings (*trois personnages primitivement*) integral to, but distinct
from, him.[14] The Bambara concept of God is thus multiple and
hypostatized as divinities, *Faro, Nyalé, N'domadyiri,* who perme-
ate elemental forces — water, wind, earth, and fire. Humankind
(qua Bambara being) *embodies* God's dissonance: human beings
"speak" the Word in myriad ways. Insufflated by the Word, the
human body itself is thus laden with cosmic significance.[15] The
liver, bladder, spleen, genitals, head, ears, eyes, nostrils circulate
the cosmic Word. Spoken virtue promotes health; duplicity proffers
dysfunction — all through the workings of one's mouth. The mouth
thus turns one inside out; one is naked as one's *spirit* is exposed as
one speaks wisely or contrary to wisdom and knowledge.[16]

The *Tyiwara,* one of the Bambara's initiation societies, reflects
aspects of their accumulated wisdom and knowledge. The *Tyiwara*
is open to males and females (the other societies are exclusively
male). In his book *The Religion, Spirituality, and Thought of Traditional Africa,* Zahan writes that the *Tyiwara* "is a synthesis of
man from the perspective of the activity of his hands. This enables
us to grasp the aptness of the connection drawn between this *dyo*
[initiation society] and the shoulder, hearing, the hands, and the
stomach. Owing to the fecundating power of received speech, the
ear is directly connected to human achievements brought about by
the other organs of this correlative set."[17] Hearing is action; the
Tyiwara is thus completely centered on the narration of the work
of the sun (male) and the earth (female) as construed in terms of

the farmer. In sum, this society's reigning body part, the ear, signifies the pulling of nourishment from the land on the model of cosmic and theistic principles responsible for human life itself.[18]

The *Tyiwara*, which I find to be a continuum of the domestic non-slave society discussed in chapter two, holds that grain grows by the strength of one's shoulders and the dexterity of one's hands. The fetus grows by the strength of one's organs, themselves dependent on shoulders and hands. The fetus and grain live in a symbiotic relationship — neither can live without the other. Life grows from the womb and depends on grain for its viability, while grain depends on tomorrow's hands and shoulders for its viability.[19] Agriculture and procreation thus signify the hominization of the cosmos. In living from the cosmic other, humankind masters its rhythms — "makes" the sun inseminate the earth out of a suffering (drought, famine, war) that strengthens the spirit. The *Tyiwara* thus "spiritualizes" the symmetry of the human being and the cosmic other through work, gestation, and cultivation. The life of the world is the life of humankind: shoulders, "ears that hear," hands, and stomach accent a cosmic truth: The germinating seed *works* inside the earth and the womb. Gestating life, itself a laboring seed, depends on the transformation of life-sustaining grain in the human being so that the community can be "unchained and demanding."

From the perspective of the Africana spirituality with which I am concerned — which involves a focus "on *theoretical* questions raised by struggles over ideas in African cultures and their *hybrid* forms" in the Diaspora — the affinity between the *Tyiwara*'s cosmic work and Morrison's antelope-dance poetry is remarkable: "They shifted shapes and became something other. Some unchained, demanding other."[20] The dancers' horns spring irrepressibly from their "head" in the same way that grain springs intrepidly from the earth. In becoming demanding in that way, in asserting their otherness, the slave community rebelled against the people who had enslaved them. Indeed, the Africans' dogged practice of whatever they could salvage of their African cultures was a significant factor in the history of slave revolts in the United States.

The Stono Rebellion (1739), for instance, which occurred during the period in which the Africans flooded South Carolina, is a prime example of the link between African values and rebellion. While mostly Angolans rather than Bambara peopled the Rebellion, the animus was African nonetheless. According to an eighteenth-century eyewitness account, "They [the rebellious]

halted in a field and set to dancing, Singing and beating Drums
to draw more Negroes to them."[21] Toni Morrison subtly con-
jures those very modalities: "Of that place where [Sethe] was
born...she remembered only song and dance....Oh but when
they sang." Neither the song nor the dance was American. Both,
moreover, call to mind Peter Wood's sense that "the Negro majority, through persistent and varied resistance to the constraints
of the slave system, brought South Carolina closer to the edge of
upheaval than historians have been willing to concede."[22]

That Sethe recalls the antelope dance during her escape from
Sweet Home, in addition, is highly significant because she was
herself in the throes of rebellion. Sethe charged, bravely escaped.
She had sent her children ahead of her to Cincinnati, Ohio, and
was bent on joining them. That Sethe remembers the antelope
dance during her escape suggests, moreover, that though *she* felt
she would die of pain, stress, and exhaustion "in wild onions,"
her baby, the *African* American in utero, the little antelope who
"rammed [Sethe] with horns and pawed the ground of her womb
with impatient hooves," foreshadows the triumph of a dogged
strength. The baby's will to become an "unchained demanding
other," her will to survive, to be born, to reincarnate an African
value, is as rebellious as her ancestor was. Sethe's mother, who had
"the bit so many times she smiled...[w]hen she wasn't smiling,"
was hanged, along with many others.[23] I think they were lynched
for trying to be unchained and demanding, for fomenting a revolt
against the plantation owners.

My intent is not to insist that Morrison had the Bambara
in mind. Rather, given Lewis Gordon's definition of Africana
thought — the focus "on *theoretical* questions raised by struggles over ideas in African cultures and their *hybrid* forms" in the
Diaspora — my intent is to take seriously Morrison's Africana per-
ceptions as a "good violence" against American Africanism. I also
am taking seriously Morrison's remark that the celebrated richness
of her writing "is what the reader gets and brings him or herself.
That's part of the way in which the tale is told. The folk tales are
told in such a way that whoever is listening is in it and can shape
it and figure it out. It's not over just because it stops. It lingers and
it's passed on. It's passed on and somebody else can alter it later."[24]

Whoever is listening is in it and can shape it and figure it out:
Sethe's experience of the antelope dance took place somewhere
on a large plantation in Carolina or Louisiana. Her reference to

Carolina makes me think of South Carolina, because South Carolina from the colonial period until the Civil War was dense with African-born slaves. As historian Sterling Stuckey observes in his book *Slave Culture: Nationalist Theory and the Foundations of Black America*, that African-born density was owed to the fact that "the South Carolina slave trade was...intense and lasted until the outbreak of the Civil War." There, "tales of the traumatizing experience of the middle passage...have been retained in the folk memory of South Carolina blacks."[25] According to Philip Curtin, in his book *The Atlantic Slave Trade: A Consensus*, "The South Carolina planters...preferred above all to have slaves from the Senegambia, which meant principally Bambara and Malinké from the interior at this period."[26] Joseph Holloway also points out that South Carolina slavers preferred "Guinea" blacks: "Wolofs and other Mandes, such as Bambara, Fulani, and Susus."[27] Veiled history, for the cultures of the Africans are underexposed in the United States, thus imposes a discussion of the Bambara on the novel and stimulates Africana spirituality. Remember that I have defined such spirituality as being in part the upholding of the memory of "third persons," who include the victims of the Middle Passage. Morrison herself states that such spirituality is part of her agenda in *Beloved:* "The gap between Africa and Afro-America and the gap between the living and the dead and the gap between the past and the present do not exist. It's bridged for us by our responsibility for people no one's even assumed responsibility for. They...died en route. Nobody knows their names, and nobody thinks about them. In addition to that, they never survived in the lore; there are no songs or dances or tales of these people."[28] *Beloved* corrects that void by bridging the gap between Africa and Afro-America.

Morrison's commitment to the ancestors in *Beloved* complements her critique of American Africanism as found in her *Playing in the Dark*. She has shown that white Americans celebrate their "Spirit," qua American Africanism, through metonymic displacement: "Color coding and other physical traits...displace rather than signify the Africanists character" so that whites might dream that whites are universal.[29] Schoolteacher, Sethe's master, exemplified such displacement. He instructed his nephews to write down Sethe's "animal" characteristics (her "wool" perhaps), next to her human ones. ("Put her human characteristics on the left; her animal ones on the right. And don't forget to line them up."[30]) Sethe overheard schoolteacher's "science," and while she didn't know at that moment what "characteristics" meant, she knew she was in trouble: A white who would so thoroughly chattelize her as to list her animal parts would sell her children before too long, and that revelation led her to join the planned escape from Sweet Home, the farm over which schoolteacher ruled.

Given the novel's presentation of the way past experiences figure intimately, if unconsciously, into a person's present, it is not hard to imagine that Sethe's resistance to schoolteacher's American Africanism was rooted in her memory of the antelope dance. Somewhere in the recesses of her mind, the memory of the plantation where she was born was strong enough to counter schoolteacher's displacement of her humanity. The antelope thus strengthened her humanity rather than displaced it: "*Oh* but when they *sang*. And *oh* but when they *danced*....They shifted shapes and became... some *unchained* demanding other." An *African* Americanism made an *American* Africanism intolerable.

Morrison reveals through the antelope dance that the African heritage empowers blacks to negate the "master narrative that spoke *for* Africans and their descendants, or *of* them."[31] That heritage, the Bambara-like spirituality, provides insight into American Africanism by deterring "the critical gaze from the racial object to the racial subject [i.e., "schoolteacher"]; from the described and imagined to the describers and imaginers; from the serving to the served." The *Tyiwara*, however speculatively employed here, strengthens that Africana agenda as it brings to light a point from *Beloved*: "Whitepeople believed that whatever the manners, under every dark skin was a jungle. Swift unnavigable waters, swinging screaming baboons, sleeping snakes, red gums ready for their sweet white blood.... But it wasn't the jungle blacks brought with them to this place from the other (livable) place. It was the jungle white-folks planted in them."[32] The antelope dance "wasn't the jungle blacks brought with them to this place from the other (livable) place." The jungle in question, that is, American Africanism, "was the jungle whitefolks planted in them."

Four other *Africanist* characters — Sixo, Paul D, Baby Suggs, and Beloved herself — signify the other livable place. Sixo, one of the Sweet Home slaves, slipped off into the woods at night to dance, to open his bloodlines. He refused to speak English except for the most serviceable of utterances — "Not move!" he says to his woman — because he found "no future in it." Before schoolteacher shot him dead, Sixo sang his warrior's song in

words his friend, Paul D, could not understand. But "he understood the sound: hatred so loose it was juba."[33] Sixo's rejection of
the Anglo-Saxon language, nocturne communions with the forest,
and rebellious "un-Negro tongue" all attest to the spirituality —
the face — of "that *other* livable place." Morrison's reference
to Sixo's "indigo" complexion, and the name itself, Sixo, like
the *Amistad*'s Cinque, also reveal that Sixo survived the Middle
Passage.

Paul D, himself a central figure in the novel, is also a trace of the
African heritage. In thinking about the depth of his emasculation
by schoolteacher and others, Paul D wonders what his fate would
have been "in Sixo's country, or his mother's? Or, God help him on
the boat."[34] Although he is not a saltwater black, he is nonetheless
a casualty of the Middle Passage.

The third face is Baby Suggs, Sethe's mother-in-law. Morrison
states in an interview that "Baby Suggs came here out of one of
those ships."[35] The community called the African-born Baby Suggs
"holy" because she spoke what one character, Stamp Paid, called
"the Word" and what Baby herself called "the Call." Her Call ex-
horted the community to love the black body to counter the hatred
"yonder." Baby Suggs's Call thus had a powerful *political* meaning:

> Yonder they do not love your flesh. They despise it. They
> don't love your eyes; they'd just as soon pick em out. No
> more do they love the skin on your back. Yonder they
> flay it. And O my people they do not love your hands.
> Those they only use, tie, bind, chop off and leave empty.
> Love your hands! Love them. Raise them up and kiss them.
> Touch others with them, pat them together, stroke them on
> your face 'cause they don't love that either. *You* got to love
> it, *you!*[36]

Colorless men, however, provoke her daughter-in-law to butcher
her beloved flesh within the veil. Sethe's "bloodspill" so depresses
Baby Suggs that she refuses to Call. She concludes that God is
like "whitepeople," who forbid blacks the simple pleasure of living contentedly in their flesh. Indeed, "God puzzled her and she
was too ashamed of Him to say so."[37]

Morrison informs us that Beloved "is a spirit...she is what
Sethe thinks she is, her child returned from the dead. And she
must function like that in the text."[38] Yet Beloved "is also another kind of dead which is not spiritual but flesh."[39] Beloved "is a
survivor from a true, factual slave ship. She speaks the language,

a traumatized language, of her own experience." For Morrison, "the language of both experiences — death and the Middle Passage — is the same."[40] Beloved is thus spirit *and* flesh, living *and* dead, Sethe's daughter *and* the living memory of the Middle Passage. Beloved vocalizes her Middle Passage experience as follows: "There will never be a time when I am not crouching and watching others who are crouching too...some who eat nasty themselves...I do not eat...the men without skin bring us their morning water to drink." She recalls people who want to die, who are "trying to leave [their] bodies behind," and the sheer density of the cramped "quarters"; a dead man is "on [her] face." She recalls the utterly exhausting sickness: "In the beginning we could vomit now we...cannot."[41]

Critic Deborah Horvitz argues that Beloved is both the reincarnation of the American baby and Sethe's African mother. For if "death and the Middle Passage evoke the same language," if "they are the same existence," they are both "experienced by the multiple-identified Beloved."[42] For Horvitz, then, as for Morrison herself, Beloved is the memory of Africa, "the place where the long grass opens," the memory of the slave ship, "the crouching place," *and* the angry casualty of the Fugitive Slave Act. Through her, "the gap is bridged between America and Africa, the past and the present, the dead and the living, the flesh and the spirit."[43] So Sethe's mother (my "Bambara" woman), Sethe herself and her spirit-daughter, Beloved, signify a mother-daughter bridge under constant threat of implosion.

Elizabeth House, on the other hand, holds that Beloved is but an actual slave-ship survivor. Her bizarre behavior and demonic disposition attest to her trauma: "From Beloved's disjointed thoughts, her stream-of-consciousness rememberings...a story can be pieced together that describes how white slave traders, 'men without skin,' captured the girl and her mother as the older woman picked flowers in Africa." Beloved thus recounts her own claustrophobic horrors, physical deprivations, and the myriad fatalities she witnessed, including her mother's, who cast herself into the Atlantic.[44]

In sum, *Beloved*'s Africana faces — Sixo, Paul D, Baby Suggs, Beloved — melt the veil with an intensity that dazzles and burns: "The struggle [these faces] can threaten *presupposes* the transcendence of expression" — a vitality burns through the distortions of an American dream.[45]

God's Puzzling Love

In burning through American Africanism, *Beloved* leaves me with the "torn-asunderness" of Baby Sugg's theodicy — the problem of the white man's religion: *God puzzled her and she was too ashamed of Him to say so.* This dialogue between Stamp Paid and Baby Suggs heightens one's sense of Baby's *aporia:*

> "You blaming God. . . . That's what you doing."
> "No, Stamp, I ain't."
> "You saying the whitefolks won?"
> "I'm saying they came in my yard."
> "You saying nothing counts."
> "I'm saying they came in my yard."
> "Sethe's the one did it."
> "And if she hadn't?"
> "You saying God give up? Nothing left for us but pour out our own blood?"
> "I'm saying they came in my yard."
> "You punishing Him, ain't you."
> "Not like He punish me."[46]

That Baby Suggs is ashamed of the God she thinks has punished her is appropriate. Only her resurrection, the eschatological intensification of her Call, will lead her to praise him. Jesus may have overcome his death on the cross, but as William Jones has pointed out, "the interval between cross and resurrection was by no means a millennium."[47] The Baby Suggs of yesterday knows no such resurrection. Until the fruition of the resurrection from the dead, or the resurrection of the dead (1 Cor 15:20–27) — whichever would apply to Baby Suggs — her *aporia* remains "a hot thing." And so does Beloved's. To remember her, to mourn her severed flesh, is to touch bases with the millions like her: black, "aborted," crushed, spit out. White Americans are especially allergic to her story. "So they [all] forgot her. Like an unpleasant dream during troubling sleep."[48]

Yet Morrison's epigraph to the novel — "I will call them my people, which were not my people; and her beloved, which was not beloved" (Rom 9:25) — raises a question that may awaken us: What if the form of God, that is, "schoolteacher" and others, conceptualizes "the other altogether differently — according to an alterity of which a few traits were traced up to now — as an incessant putting in question . . . of the priority and the quiet of the

Same, like the burning without consumption of an inextinguishable flame"?[49] As a "hot thing" within the veil, this "incessant putting in question" can be stated as follows: "Must...all of human history...fulfill itself dialectically...through...the final triumph of *identification* in the Absolute Idea" qua the form of God — "the very idea of completion or the ultimate"?[50] Must God be the master's image and no one else's? Must the Religion deify "the usurpation carried out by the conquerors," that is, the universal historians? Must universal history record "enslavement, forgetting the life that struggles against slavery"?[51]

Chapter 5

God Is Nobody's Toy

James Baldwin's Rejection of a Nullifying Double Standard

> God is . . . not anybody's toy.
> — JAMES BALDWIN[1]

Must . . . all of human history . . . fulfill itself dialectically . . . through . . . the final triumph of identification in the Absolute Idea?[2] That is, must God's form negate African Americans to be "Spirit"? Why can't God be "a means of liberation and not a means to control others"?[3] If God is not a means to control others, if, as Levinas put it, "the social relationship is worth more than [the master's] enjoyment of [himself]" — then there is an alternative to the God who puzzled Baby Suggs.[4]

"The Threshing Floor"

James Baldwin began to discover this alternative in Mount Calvary of the Pentecostal Faith, a Harlem church led by the famous preacher Mother Horn. Baldwin wrote of his discovery in his novel *Go Tell It on the Mountain* and best-selling long essay *The Fire Next Time*. In the novel, the discovery takes place during a tarrying service on the Saturday night of John Grime's fourteenth birthday. The saints filtered into the Temple of the Fire Baptized, the fictionalized reference to Mother Horn's church. The seriousness of their lives frightened John: all the hurt of the Southland and all the bitter disappointment of the promised land (Harlem). "[His] heart grew cold. The Lord was riding on the wind" that night.[5] "All over the church there was only the sound, more awful than the deepest silence, of the prayers of the saints of God."[6]

Before he knew it, John succumbed to the "Frenzy."[7] John found himself on the floor of the church: "Dust was in his nostrils, sharp and terrible, and the feet of the saints, shaking the floor beneath him, raised small clouds of dust that filmed his mouth. He heard their cries, so far, so high above him — he could never rise that far. He was like a rock, a dead man's body, a dying bird, fallen from an awful height; something that had no power of itself, any more, to turn."[8] In *The Fire Next Time,* Baldwin put it this way: After Mother Horn

> had finished preaching, everything came roaring, screaming, crying out, and I fell to the ground before the altar. It was the strangest sensation I have ever had in my life — up to that time, or since. I had not known that it was going to happen, or that it could happen. One moment I was on my feet, singing and clapping and, at the same time, working out in my head a plot of a play I was working on then; the next moment, with no transition, no sensation of falling, I was on my back, with the lights beating down into my face and all the vertical saints above me. I did not know what I was doing down so low, or how I got there. And the anguish that filled me cannot be described. It moved in me like one of those floods that devastate countries, tearing everything down, tearing down children from their parents and lovers from each other, and making everything an unrecognizable waste.[9]

In *Go Tell It on the Mountain,* Baldwin informs us that his vulnerability made him scream in "bewildered terror"; "he felt himself turning...as though God's toe had touched him lightly."[10]

The Americanness of John's vertigo, the consciousness that he better surface lest he "become like all the other niggers," kept him from total oblivion even as he sank deeper into the experience. Still, his fear of becoming a statistic within the veil could not at that point overcome the contemptuous "God" who turned him. His fear of being trapped in the ghetto "was as far back as he could go, but the secret of the turning" — "God's toe" — "was farther back, in darkness," and so he "was going down."[11] "To the bottom of the sea, the bowels of the earth, to the heart of the fiery furnace? Into a dungeon deeper than hell, into a madness louder than the grave? What trumpet sound would awaken him, what hand would lift him up?"[12] If you would allow me to quilt *Mountain* and *Beloved* together, could the puzzling God, who embarrassed Baby Suggs, John's ancestor from a certain inverted "canonical" perspective — raise a black body from that place underneath the grave, which is death itself? "For [John] knew, as he was struck again, and screamed again, his throat like burning ashes, and as he [was] turned again, his body hanging from him like a useless weight, a heavy, rotting carcass, that if he were not lifted he would never rise."[13] "Then death is real, John's soul said, and Death will have his moment."[14]

Facing Death, John encountered his ancestors, who "filled the grave, like a thousand wings beating the air." They "began to murmur — a terrible sound — and John's ears trembled."[15] For John *hears* their "rage that had no language, weeping with no voice — which yet spoke . . . to John's startled soul, of boundless melancholy, of the bitterest patience, and the longest night, of the deepest water, the strongest chains, the most cruel lash; of humility most wretched, the dungeon most absolute, of love's bed defiled, and birth dishonored, and most bloody, unspeakable, sudden death."[16] John realized that "the darkness hummed with murder: the body in the water, the body in the fire, the body on the tree."[17]

On the floor, face to face with those Morrison has called in *Beloved* the "black and angry dead," John then had a vision of Holy Communion. Bringing John 13 to mind, the nullified "broke . . . flat unsalted bread, which was the body of the Lord, and drank from a heavy silver cup the scarlet wine of his blood." The saints then washed each other's feet; but *their* feet, having walked the earth of a Christian nation that had practically excluded them from salvation, were unwashable:

> Many washings only turned the crystal water red; and someone cried: *"Have you been to the river? . . .* and the multitude was there. And now they had undergone a change; their robes were ragged, and stained with the road they had traveled, and stained with unholy blood; the robes of some barely covered their nakedness; and some indeed were naked. And some stumbled on the smooth stones at the river's edge, for they were blind; and some crawled with a terrible wailing, for they were lame; some did not cease to pluck at their flesh, which was rotten with running sores. All struggled to get to the river, in a dreadful hardness of heart: the strong struck down the weak, the ragged spat on the naked, the naked cursed the blind, the blind crawled over the lame. And someone cried: *"Sinner, do you love my Lord?"*[18]

Before discovering whether the river would be as nonsalvific for black folk as the basin of foot-washing water — before he discovered that the God who puzzled Baby Suggs, and had turned him, was incapable of admitting the black body into "heaven" — before Death could claim him for ever and ever — John "saw the Lord — for a moment only; and the darkness, for a moment only, was filled with a light he could not bear. Then, in a moment, he was set free; his tears sprang as from a fountain; his heart, like a fountain of waters, burst. Then he cried: "Oh, blessed Jesus! Oh, Lord Jesus! Take me through!"[19]

"Jesus," his own flesh and blood in all the likeness of the living, had been responsible for *him,* had not forsaken him in the place where the "worm does not die" (Mark 9:48). In rising toward Jesus, whose Spirit is always present in one person's ethical responsibility for another, John discovered in those who loved him, who had "prayed him through," the alternative to the nullifying "God" of the antiblack river below.

In *The Devil Finds Work,* another long essay that reflects on his threshing floor experience, Baldwin writes:

> There was a rite in our church, called *pleading the blood.* When the sinner fell on his face before the altar, the soul of the sinner then found itself locked in battle with Satan: or, in the place of Jacob, wrestling with the angel. All of the forces of Hell rushed in to claim the soul which had just been astonished by the light of the love of God. The soul in torment turned this way and that, yearning, equally for the light and for the darkness: yearning out of agony for reconciliation — and for rest: for this agony is compounded by an unimaginable, unprecedented, unspeakable fatigue. Only the saints who had passed through this fire — the incredible horror of fainting in the spirit — had the power to intercede, to "plead the blood," to bring the embattled and mortally endangered soul "through." The pleading of the blood was a plea to whosoever had loved us enough to spill his blood for us, that he might sprinkle the soul with his love once more, to give us power over Satan, and the love and courage to live out our days.... I had been prayed through, and I, then, prayed others through: had testified to having been born again, and, then, helped others to be born again.[20]

My Dungeon Shook and My Chains Fell Off

After his threshing floor experience, James Baldwin spent a fair bit of his teenage years as a preacher in the church that had "saved" him. He had to leave the church, however, to actualize his redemption. Time, hindsight, allowed him to see why: the God he had proclaimed from the pulpit, the God who had turned him while he was on the floor, was white. Baldwin realized that he had felt that way, quite unwillingly, when he writhed on the dusty Harlem floor. Even then he wondered (with Baby Suggs, if you will): "If His [God's] love was so great, and if He loved all his children, why were we, the blacks, cast down so far? Why?" Despite his short-lived vocation as an evangelist, Baldwin confides to his readers that he found no answer "on the floor — not *that* answer, anyway — and [remember, he] was on the floor all night."[21]

He experienced "relief," however, which confused him until he figured out why he had achieved it "in a fashion at once so pagan and so desperate — in a fashion at once so unspeakably old and so unutterably new."[22] He realized that the paganism, the singing, the percussive tambourines, and the memory of possession trance, the traces of his African ancestors in those who had prayed him through, were what relieved him. The black church's captivity to the God who had turned him, however, accounted for why Baldwin felt that his career as an evangelist was a dead end. As he put it in *The Fire Next Time,* "The blood of the Lamb had not cleansed me in any way whatever. I was just as black as I had been the day I was born."[23] He realized that his descent, the pagan desperation traceable to his African ancestors, was his truth. He discovered that there was no need for him to practice a Religion that privileged whites. He realized that it was healthier for him to embrace his blackness and celebrate its cultural richness derived from Africa.

What Du Bois called the "Music" and the "Frenzy," which he linked to the memory of Africa in his seminal essay "Of the Faith of the Fathers," moved Baldwin even after he left the church. He writes that he had "never seen anything to equal the fire and excitement that sometimes, without warning, fill a church, causing the church...to 'rock.' "[24] As Baldwin ponders the fact that he had "been born again" and had "helped others to be born again," he surfaces the precious thing he has mined from the recesses of the veil, the dusty store-front floor: "The blacks did not so much use Christian symbols as recognize them — recognize them for what they were before the Christians [i.e., the masters] came along —

and, thus, reinvested these symbols with their original energy. The proof of this, simply, is the continued existence and authority of the blacks: it is through the creation of the black church that an unwritten, dispersed, and violated inheritance has been handed down."[25]

Baldwin has not only affirmed Baby Sugg's Call and Sethe's antelope dance, he has also affirmed Du Bois's face, specifically his book *The Souls of Black Folk*. Du Bois writes that the spirituality of the black church "was not at first by any means Christian nor definitely organized; rather it was an adaptation and mingling of heathen [*sic*] rites among the members of each plantation, and roughly designated as Voodooism."[26] As I see it, Baldwin is arguing that those African roots enabled the blacks to reinvest Christian symbols with their original energy. By "original" one does not mean that the antelope dance through which Sethe remembers her African-born mother is *older* than Christianity. Given the Africana spirituality with which I am concerned, it is rather the case that such "voodooism" is closer to the gospel's humane God than the Religion that required blacks to abandon their heritage.

That many black Christians have been unable to celebrate the African heritage as a spirituality compatible with Christian symbols sheds light on Baldwin's view that "the principles governing the rites and customs" of the black churches "did not differ from" those "governing the rites and customs of other churches, white." Baldwin calls these principles "Blindness, Loneliness, and Terror."[27] Terror has been especially prevalent in the black church to the extent that it has reflected how the Africans' progeny had come to be Christian in the first place: through the fear of damnation rather than the love of God. Their fear both propitiated the master, always ready to punish disobedient blacks, and intensified their resentment of him. Blacks were afraid *not* to recite the Apostles' Creed their masters taught them, though blacks' faithfulness excised their masters from salvation *and* carried the suspicion that the Lord's Supper was inefficacious for blacks. In light of that contradiction, Baldwin writes that

> the vision people hold of the world to come is but a reflection, with predictable wishful distortions, of the world in which they live. And this did not only apply to Negroes, who were no more "simple" or "spontaneous" or "Christian" than anybody else — who were merely more oppressed. In the same way that we, for white people, were cursed forever,

white people were, for us, the descendants of Cain. And the passion with which we loved the Lord was a measure of how deeply we feared and distrusted and, in the end, hated almost all strangers, always, and avoided and despised ourselves.[28]

Levinas provides a clue as to why. He writes: "In our spiritual heritage, love of one's neighbor . . . would at best be only the second commandment, after the love of God. And that ethics, according to the theologians, would never equal the true essence of the relation to God. . . . At the religious level, morality would be considered something we have moved beyond."[29] In sublating the second commandment to the first one, the pious have been blinded by their "identification in the Absolute Idea," by their self-deification on the one hand and self-negation on the other. Baldwin's threshing floor experience freed him from that master-slave dialectic, which forced him to conclude that if "the concept of God has any validity or any use, it can only be to make us larger, freer, and more loving. If God cannot do this, then it is time we got rid of Him."[30]

The African Heritage and Our Concept of God

Baldwin's attempts to liberate the concept of God from the narrow principles of the Religion continued to push him to struggle with the African heritage. His essay "Princes and Powers" reveals his alienation from Africa. In this essay, he rejects Leopold Senghor's claim that Richard Wright's *Black Boy* is an African autobiography in essence. According to Baldwin, *Black Boy* "had nothing to do with Africa" because the novel had been written in English and thus hailed from Greece and Rome: "Its form, psychology, moral attitude, preoccupations, in short, its cultural validity, were all forces which had nothing to with Africa. Or was it simply that we had been rendered unable to recognize Africa in it."[31] In that same volume of essays, *Nobody Knows My Name*, Baldwin's "East River, Downtown" argues that Africa's devolution to "self rule" has had the effect of liberating black Americans from white America's image of them. According to Baldwin, Africa's independence — a misnomer in any case — has revealed that blacks "were not merely the descendants of slaves in a white, Protestant, and Puritan country: they were also related to kings and princes in an ancestral homeland, far away. And this has proved to be a great antidote to the poison of self-hatred."[32] In this essay, Baldwin tends to romanticize the African heritage.

In truth, many kings and princes sold the ancestors to the Europeans and the Americans. While a few of us may be of royal descent, we mostly belong to the history of the African poor — the nonfree laborers: prisoners of war and the indebted. Baldwin acknowledges that truth in the 1984 preface of *Notes of a Native Son* as he writes of "the chiefs who sold Africans into slavery." Still, he lets the chiefs off the hook in stating that they "could not have had any idea that this slavery was meant to endure forever, or at least *a thousand years.*"[33] In the early part of the nineteenth century, the Asante monarch Osei Bonsu seemed to know very well what he was doing. Lamenting the suppression of the Atlantic trade, he said:

> If I fight a king and kill him when he is insolent, then certainly I must have his gold, and his slaves, and the people are mine too. Do not the white kings act like this? Because I hear the old men say, that before I conquered Fantee and killed the Braffoes and the kings, that white men came in great ships, and fought and killed many people; and then they took the gold and slaves to the white country: and sometimes they fought together. That is all the same as these black countries. The great God and the fetische made war for strong men everywhere, because then they can pay plenty of gold and proper sacrifice.... Now you must tell my master [that is, George III of England] that these slaves can work for him, and if he wants 10,000 he can have them. And if he wants fine handsome girls and women to give his captains, I can send him great numbers.[34]

Would such a "chief," so mindful of his gold and his honor, call the whole thing off because African slaves had become American chattel?

African complicity in the Middle Passage does not, however, diminish the problem of the Religion — its role in the making of the American Negro. This, after all, is Baldwin's point: any religion based on the damnation of others is too high-priced for the dammed. And when Christianity is such a rock-bottom religion, one has recourse to an alternative — a fecund spirituality. According to Baldwin's biographer, David Leeming, Baldwin indeed discovered the roots of that spirituality during his visit to Africa in 1962. He discovered that "his external 'white consciousness,' his sense of the appropriate instilled in him by a long history as a minority race, was challenged by a physical representation of a way of perceiving that had its source in prehistoric times, before humans began to think about who or what they were."[35] Baldwin thus discovered in Africa — "its exoticism, its marketplace scents and sounds" — an analogue of what had helped him survive and challenge the hatefulness of white supremacy: "something of the depth, the ability to touch, the willingness to accept the 'stink of love' that he had chastised his nation for suppressing. Africa in all of its turmoil, in all of its pain, was teeming with the essence of what it was on the most basic level to be human, and Africa was, above all, black."[36] Why, then, asks Baldwin, "should I abandon my gods for yours? For I *know* my gods are real: they have enabled me to withstand you."[37] Baldwin's "gods" symbolize his face, his truth, his rejection of a double standard — his double-consciousness of why, precisely, human relief had to be achieved in a fashion at once so pagan and so desperate.

In his book *No Name in the Street,* Baldwin's love of his gods bears an affinity to Du Bois's double-consciousness; but whereas Du Bois explained his double-consciousness in terms of our being American and Negro, Baldwin surmises that "the most accurate term, now, for this history, this particular and peculiar danger, as well as for all persons produced out of it and struggling in it, is: Afro-American."[38] For Baldwin, Afro-American connects "two currently undefined proper nouns" — for Africa "is still chained to Europe, and exploited by Europe."[39] Africa, then, cannot be itself until "the many millions of people on the continent of Africa control their land and their resources," until "the African personality flowers or genuinely African institutions flourish and reveal Africa as she is."[40] America also "poses as profound and dangerous a mystery for human understanding as does the fabled dark continent of Africa."[41] Whereas Africa is "a cradle and a potential," the United States — "that part of the North American continent which calls itself, arrogantly enough, *America*" — has not yet understood that its abuse of its *own* African people is its true reflection and not its claim to be the leader of the free world.

To place these enigmas side by side, Africa and America, to contemplate "the history and possible future of Africa, and the history and possible future of America" — is to realize that "something is illuminated of the nature, the depth and the tenacity of the great war between black and white life styles here [in the United States]. Something is suggested of the nature of fecundity, the nature of sterility, and one realizes that it is by no means a simple matter to know which is which: the one can very easily resemble the other."[42] These two warring ideals, fecundity and sterility, take on peculiar force in "Afro-Americans," one dark body, for we must discern which is which. Not to entrench the color line, but to understand what is fecund and what is sterile. For fecundity, dogged strength within the veil, discovers the mysterious love of God everywhere in the world. Even in "pagan" Africa — for "God is...not anybody's toy."[43] And as for sterility, well, what does sterility want if not a nullifying double standard?

Part Three

Africana Spirituality

Progenies of the Middle Passage
and Their Implications for Today

Chapter 6

Questions Louder Than Drums
This Discomfort

Questions louder than drums begin beating in the mind, and one realizes that what is called civilization lives first of all in the mind, has the mind above all as its province, and that the civilization, or its rudiments, can continue to live long after its externals have vanished — they can never entirely vanish from the mind. These questions — they are too vague for questions, this excitement, this discomfort — concern the nature of any inheritance and the means by which that inheritance is handed down. — JAMES BALDWIN[1]

James Baldwin has asserted that Africa and America signify a conflict "between black and white life styles." For Baldwin, the conflict concerns the distinction between sterility and fecundity and the danger that one can easily mistake fecundity for its sterile counterpart and vice versa.[2] In order to avoid confusion, Baldwin has argued that fecundity has to do with the black lifestyle molded by the "dark gods" rather than the God who turned him on the threshing floor.[3]

If Africa is the source of the dark gods, then African Americans in quest of fecundity might be wise to consult Africans about those gods as they might prove helpful in understanding what Baldwin has called "the depth and the tenacity of the great war between black and white life styles" in the United States. After all, we are an African people, survivors of the Middle Passage, and that fact goes a long way toward accounting for our conflicts with white Americans.

Sterility, Fecundity, and the Passage of Time

One of the Africans who has instructed me the most about those conflicts is the Nigerian writer and activist Wole Soyinka. The

African Americans who have "made pilgrimages to the isle of Goree, visited the forts and slaves monuments of Accra, Cape Coast, Dar es Salaam and Zanzibar, traversed the tunnels and dungeons where their ancestors had trodden, and agonized over what gods they had failed to placate to bring down such a calamity on their heads" have moved him.[4] According to Soyinka, such agony is "as much a part of our history, we, the stay-at-homes...as it is of those who were forcibly displaced."[5] Facing a relic of the Middle Passage, such as the Elmina Castle that I mentioned earlier, Soyinka expresses his kinship to African Americans in terms of a question: What is *slave?* "What humanity is it? What, precisely, is its ontology?"[6] His question is akin to Du Bois's "What does it mean to be a problem?"

Soyinka "answers" his question by asserting that the ontology in question is foreign to Africa: "The spirituality of the black continent, as attested, for instance, in the religion of the *orisa* [the Yoruba gods of Nigeria and the Americas], abhors...coercion or exclusion, and recognizes...spiritual urgings as attributes of the complex disposition of godhead. *Tolerance* is synonymous with the spirituality of the black continent, *intolerance* is anathema!"[7] But this, he offers, "is never sufficient to silence those who can only read the *spirituality* of a continent and a people in the skyline of church steeples and the minarets of mosques."[8]

Given what we know about the Asante slavers, King Osei Bonsu, and others, and given the history of the African poor, which is a history of caste hierarchy and even immolation of human beings (the slaves), Soyinka's view is problematic. Yet he is hardly the first polemicist to uphold the goodness of a spirituality despite evidence to the contrary. He has good reason to be critical of the "continuing tradition of denial of, and disrespect toward, a continent's own spirituality."[9] Indeed, his question — What is *slave?* What humanity is it? — raises many questions about Christianity's institutionalization of "slave humanity" and sanctification of the master. In his implicit critique of Hegel's *The Philosophy of History*, Soyinka points out:

> Unlike the idealists of History, for whom History is an impersonal totem, a utopian projection thrust into the future by the unstoppable potency of some abstracted, extrapolated Will, and, nearer still, unlike the materialist (Marxist) revision of that persuasion, whose restitution of the human entity to history is no less reductive of that very entity, rendering it

subservient to its own utopian vision, we insist on the deter-
minant and purpose of history as the human entity in and for
itself, even as asserted by W. E. B. Du Bois.... "We often forget that each unit in the mass is a throbbing human soul.... It
loves and hates, it toils and tires, it laughs and weeps in bitter tears, and looks in vague and awful longing at the grim
horizon of its life."[10]

Indeed, "a throbbing human soul" realizes that civilization has not
been the province of Europe alone. Africa has civilizations too, and
African Americans' memory of them "can continue to live long
after its externals have vanished."[11]

Certainly Du Bois, Morrison, and Baldwin have surfaced traces
of those civilizations, which have intensified the conflict between
black and white lifestyles in the United States in raising the questions: Whose fecundity illumines "the nature, the depth and the
tenacity of the great war" between black and white lifestyles in
America?" Whose sterility provokes Soyinka to write that "a religion that separated humanity into the saved and the damned — the
latter being qualified for mass deportation to distant lands as beasts
of burden — can hardly be considered fundamentally compatible
with the people on whom such a choice was imposed"?[12]

Inheritances and How They Have Been Handed Down

Those questions motivated two study groups that I led to Africa
in the late 'nineties. I led the first group to Zimbabwe, and I have
already mentioned the second, a study group that I led to Ghana.
The Zimbabwe group was concerned about the racial divide in the
United States, and, initially, all of the blacks were very much interested in discovering the extent to which "dark gods" "have been
modified by the passage of time."[13] My sense is that most returned
home convinced that time has just about extinguished in them
what Soyinka has called "the spirituality of the black continent."[14]

The students were comfortable in one of the "historic"
churches, St. Peters, a United Methodist church that clergy and
laity have Africanized by translating hymns and Scripture into
Shona and using traditional drums and rattles as complements
to the piano. The Shona, a Bantu people with many dialects, are
Zimbabwe's majority. The spirituality was that of well-catechized

Protestants. I thought the comfort level dropped, however, when we visited an African independent church, with which few of the "mission" churches, that is, "historic" churches, have much to do. As one member of St. Peter's put it, "They go too far." In the independent church, Guta Rah Jehova, the "saints" lived in traditional roundhouses and held their worship services outdoors. Ironically, they used no traditional instruments. They used huge bass drums and bugles. Yet I found the music more traditional than that of the first church — more basic.

"Basic" is another word for what Soyinka calls a commencing code, "the need for preservation of the material and spiritual properties by which memory is invested."[15] Soyinka would have us respect this code — "its burdens and triumphs or, better still, its actuality, the simple fact of its anterior existence and its validity for its time."[16] "Basic," then, means that the music of Guta Rah Jehova was not as harmonic as St. Peter's; but I found it more revelatory of an intransigent identity than was the case with the Methodist church: The smooth, kinetic, traditional movement to brass and bass drums and polyrhythmic hand clapping hardly seemed like reading "the *spirituality* of a continent and a people in the skyline of church steeples." The immediacy of the sky and the earth intensified a traditional Shona demand for sacred space. In getting down to basics, these Africans satisfied an imperative that they deemed as essential for the efficacy of what was being done: the expression of their Christian faith in the primal elements that have sustained Shona people for centuries.

If the commencing code — the "preservation of the material and spiritual properties by which memory is invested" (as Soyinka put it) — was musical and spatial in the independent church, we observed its *ritualistic* implications later that week. Our host, Patrick Matsikenyiri, then warden of Africa University and director of its choir, arranged an audience with a subchief of Zimunya, a Shona clan. The chief was at least a hundred years old and remembered well what life was like before the English made Zimunya part of Southern Rhodesia (the name the English settlers had given to what the Africans now call Zimbabwe). Matsikenyiri informed us that the old chief's mother had engaged in ritual incest with a paramount chief in the latter part of the eighteenth century. The revelation discomforted the students.

My question later that evening, "Did you notice the pride the chief displayed with respect to his mother?" sparked no one to ask

why the incest had occurred. Few seemed interested in my speculation that the incest might be construed in terms of Victor Turner's
notion of "liminality," which signifies the suspension of the prevailing morality in order to fortify autochthonous institutions such
as kingship. Evans Zuesse in his *Ritual Cosmos: The Sanctification
of Life in African Religions,* which makes use of Turner's theory, points out, "the world of normality is temporarily abolished
in . . . rituals of reversal [i.e., liminality]." The "basic taboos which
help structure that world must be momentarily broken. Every such
violation," as in the incest in question, "is a symbolic sacrifice in
which the material and visible world is offered up again to the invisible transcendental forms that inspirit it."[17] Although Zuesse's
interpretation is problematic to me (it seems Platonic to me) I
agree that the incest symbolized sacrifice. Indeed, the incest, en-
acted in the late nineteenth century, probably had a bearing on the
abandoned practice of sacrificing kings.

According to Luc de Heusch's *Sacrifice in Africa,* the Kuba
people, a Bantu people like the Shona, enthroned their king by
transgressing kinship laws. He had "sexual relations with a sister and [married] a grand-niece from his own matrilineal family
group."[18] Tradition deemed the king to be "the formidable master
of natural forces" and sacrificed him as "the ultimate expression of
the prohibitions that hedge in his excessive power, his monstrous
counter-cultural nature."[19] He became a nature spirit after death,
whose power was concentrated in the pangolin, an anteater.[20] I
discovered the pertinence of the pangolin for the Shona later.

The occasion for that discovery was our visit to the son of
Zimunya's paramount chief, whom we met the day after we visited the old chief. After the chief's lecture, one of my students told
him that she felt robbed of her African heritage, was in effect put
out by the way an inheritance had been handed down to her. She
thus beseeched the chief to give her some wisdom that would help
her cope with the conflict between black and white lifestyles in
America. The chief then had his liaisons fetch a supply of pangolin "shells," that is, scales, harbored in a shed but a few yards
from where we sat. I could not help but reflect on my study of Luc
de Heusch's *Sacrifice in Africa,* which also involves a discussion of
Mary Douglas's work on the Congolese Lele, a Bantu people not
unlike the Shona and the Kuba.

For the Lele, the pangolin (*manis tricupis*) "combines the properties of aquatic, celestial and terrestrial creatures. Monoparous,

it is also the symbolic representative of moderated human reproduction in a world where fertility is teeming beyond measure."[21]
Cosmic forces — water, earth and sky — thus converge in the
small pangolin: Its scaly body is fish-like, yet it's a mammal that
lives in trees like a bird. In distinction from other land mam-
mals, moreover, the pangolin bears its young one at a time as do
most humans.[22] Edified by Mary Douglas, de Heusch explains that
the Lele's pangolin is "the absolute equivalent of the Kuba sacred
king, the regulator of the cosmic as well as of the social order."[23]
Furthermore, according to de Heusch, "The fact that the Lele as-
sociate the small pangolin with general fertility by giving it the title
'chief,' thus conferring upon it the same power that their neigh-
bors the Kuba attribute only to the sovereign, suggests that this
decidedly strange creature is capable of mapping a route for us toward the most singular of sacrificial institutions: the ritual killing
of kings."[24] In order to promote fecundity, the "chief" sacrifices itself for the village, thus strengthening reproduction. The "chief"
surrenders to the hunters: "It lets itself fall from a tree and instead of fleeing, it rolls itself into a ball and does not move. The
hunter merely has to wait until [the pangolin] unrolls itself and
lifts its head in order to kill it." According to de Heusch, then, it
is "in terms of sacrifice that one must interpret the killing and eat-
ing of this animal."[25] As a spirit of nature, the pangolin is thought
to be inexhaustible like "the royal descendants; far from ending
royalty, the sacrifice of a king assures the perpetual regeneration
of . . . power."[26]

In exposing the shells for the sake of fecundity, namely the
healing of the student's pain, the Zimunyan paramount gave
the student what still seems to me to be the heart and soul
of her anguished request for contiguity. He gave himself away
synecdochically with the "shells," thus exemplifying the fact that
the "association of the pangolin with royalty is found throughout Bantu Africa."[27] The heir to the paramount gave the student
a powerful metonym of the social cohesion he embodied. To me,
the gift was enormous. As de Heusch put it: "Is it not the ritual
function of sacred royalty to control all natural forces? The sacred
king is both at the very heart of human order, and outside it, in the
heart of nature, just like the pangolin."[28]

Without question, de Heusch's theory corresponded to what
the chief was *saying:* He told us that *he* was Zimunya, the local-
ized cosmos. He told us that he should be able to walk anywhere

in Zimunya without the slow Egyptian cobra or the swift black-mouthed mamba "hitting" him or any of his people. A "hit" would have meant that something was *wrong*. If need be, he could make it rain, especially if the spirits, the royal ancestors, favored him. Given the wealth of shells that he exposed to soothe the student's suffering, we are to understand that the spirits clearly did. The surplus of shells, metonyms of fecundity, was a sign that all was well. His gift to the student who lamented the "loss" of her African heritage, that is, the way inheritances had been handed down, was *Be well, go well!* As I reflect on it now, his gift was precisely the fecundity that illumines "the nature, the depth and the tenacity of the great war" between black and white lifestyles in America. I translate that fecundity as follows: Don't allow the Religion to define you — the meaning of your history and your connection to black Africa.

For me, part of that connection means that I must accept Africa's role in the Atlantic slave trade, which is apparently connected to the practice of regicide. Claude Meillassoux argues in his *Anthropology of Slavery: The Womb of Iron and Gold* that all slavery is based on alienation, the nullification of slaves' "right" to kinship within a society, and that the king himself symbolized that alienation. "The rituals which were inflicted on the divine king de-socialized him by reversing kinship relations: he had to eliminate, exile or kill his rival brothers. In Oyo [Nigeria], the king killed his mother, who was replaced by a fictitious mother recruited by the court from its midst."[29] According to Meillassoux, "the king sometimes had to marry his sister, which deprived him of relations of affinity."[30] In the historic kingdom of Monomotapa, itself related to the Shona, the king copulated "with a female crocodile during his enthronement, his divinity supposedly protecting him (perhaps) from this dehumanization."[31] The final indignity involved regicide, replete with the immolation of the royal court, the king's wives, and those close to him. Sacrifice thus "represented the ultimate subordination of his divinity to the true power, that of his entourage which took the decision."[32] According to Meillassoux, the king was a living mask of the elite who profited from the slave economy. "The protocol imposed on [the king], designed to increase his spiritual majesty, revealed his temporal powerlessness and his dependence. He could not leave the palace; sometimes he could not even be seen; he had to address the people through a spokesman.... When he was authorized to appear in public, he was weighted down by so much sumptuous finery and regalia that he could not move or make a gesture without help."[33]

Neither the religious (de Heusch) nor the political (Meillassoux) interpretation tells the whole truth. Both, however, have some bearing on the conflict of black and white lifestyles (on the way inheritances have been handed down). Our encounter with the Zimunyan paramount who shared the pangolins with us indicates the integrity of what Soyinka has called Africa's "commencing codes." The prince was wise and gracious. Still, the continent has been burdened by its own (autochthonous) inhumanity. Slavery in Africa, like slavery in the United States, covered up its brutality with religious pretext. If Christianity cannot be reduced to such brutality, neither can African religion. As it is, however, many African Americans, molded by a certain philosophy of history, are convinced that Africa, past and present, has been without a shred of fecundity.

For authorities on African fecundity such as Soyinka, the role that the white man's religion has played in enforcing that view is exceedingly problematic. Making claims very similar to Baldwin's regarding the way an inheritance has been handed down, Soyinka claims that Africa "was enslaved under the divine authority of the ... christian [sic] gods, their earthly plenipotentiaries, and commercial stormtroopers."[34] Chinua Achebe, another Nigerian, asserts that he would be happy if his novels, particularly those that deal with the ancestors, "did no more than teach [blacks] that their past — with all its imperfections — was not one long night of savagery from which the first Europeans acting on God's behalf delivered them."[35] Yet few of the students who had invested their time and money to come to Zimbabwe seemed interested in that perspective. It was as if the only fecundity to speak of had to be understood in terms of the African churches that distanced themselves from the independent ones and the pangolin. To what extent does that perspective reflect the sterility of blacks' acquiescence in the form of God?

The question took on added force during the trip to Ghana, part of which has already been discussed. In Ghana we visited the herbalist, the *Sumankwafo,* who serves the forest dwarfs, the *mmoatia.* According to R. S. Rattray, a pioneering scholar on traditional Asante spirituality, the

> most characteristic feature of these Ashanti [Asante] "little folk" ... is their feet, which point backwards. They are said

to be about a foot in stature, and to be of three distinct varieties: black, red, and white, and they converse by means of whistling. The black fairies *[mmoatia]* are more or less innocuous, but the white and the red *mmoatia* are up to all kind of mischief, such as stealing house-wives' palm-wine and the food left over from the previous day. The light colored *mmoatia* are also versed in the making of all manner of *suman* [charms] which they may at times be persuaded to barter to mortals.[36]

According to Rattray, "many Ashanti medicine-men," such as the herbalist who hosted us, "claim to have lived with the little folk, and to have learned all their arts of healing from them."[37] In calling on the *Sumankwafo,* a pupil of the *mmoatia,* we had gone to the boundary of culture, the threshold of nature. The scene was rustic and darkened by the heavy forest foliage.

The herbalist, the *Sumankwafo,* poured "libation," herbally treated homemade gin, to the ancestors. His assistants passed the cup around. We drank, then poured a bit for the ancestors. The assistants instructed us to shed our shoes and took us to the spirit-house, a shed — part nature, part culture. One of the assistants took us around the spirit-house and had us notice that nothing could enter from its exterior. Its interior was replete with paraphernalia that reminded me of Vodun altars blackened by sacrifice. A curtain — permeable, but dividing village and forest — split the shed in two. The assistant lifted the curtain: "Do you see anything?" "No." He had verified the solidity of the spirit-house. Anyone who entered the shed in any way other than through the front door had to be spirit. The *Sumankwafo* took the schnapps we furnished him into his mouth and blew the liquor onto the curtain three times. He then summoned the *mmoatia* three times and struck the partition three times: We heard shed-shaking knocking in threefold reply.

The *Sumankwafo's* assistant opened the partition and asked each of us individually whether we saw one of the *mmoatia.* "Do you see him?" I said yes because I *thought* I saw a *suman.* Rattray writes that a *suman,* wrongly called a fetish, "is an object which is the potential dwelling-place of a spirit or spirits of an inferior status, generally belonging to the vegetable kingdom; this object is also closely associated with the control of the powers of evil or black magic [*sic*], for personal ends."[38] As Rattray has noted, "*suman* come from the *mmoatia,* (fairies) by whom they were first made and from whom they are still obtained. You place ten cowries on a rock, go away; on your return you find your cowries gone, having been replaced by a *suman*."[39] Apparently, then, the spirit had announced his presence, taken our first offering, and left his "calling card" to inform us that more "cowries" were needed if he were to stand still.

After they had taken up another "offering," the assistants reparted the curtain and instructed us to kneel individually. I knelt and saw the "spirit" — a truly exquisite masquerade. The textile, a black-striped cloth, covered his body, while long black hair, perhaps from a primate, covered his face. The mask, textile and hair, quivered with uncanny energy, powerful but subtle, and spoke the esoteric tongue of the *mmoatia*. How did he get in there? Where was the box of fruit and candy that we had given him? How did he rock the space behind the partition with such force? And how did he throw us back a portion of the candy we had given him? And from where?

Rattray speculates, and it seems likely to me, that the *mmoatia* may well represent "the diminutive forest race," the pygmies, who inhabited the rain forest before the Asante domesticated portions of it with "un-free labor." According to historian Ivor Wilkes, moreover, rural Asante still respect the *mmoatia,* who symbolize "the farmers' early attempts to establish a satisfactory and productive niche with the forest environment."[40] The *mmoatia* thus remind us of "the most complex ecosystem on the earth" — formidable, magical. To "tame" that forest took a certain dogged strength. Until today,

> the bioclimatic system is a complex one, resting upon the maintenance of a balance between the protection and sustenance of the soil, provided by the heavy forest cover, and the threat to the soil, through the high levels of insolation and rainfall, presented by the climate. While the renewal of the cycle of the humid forest is little disturbed by the activities of human communities engaged primarily in hunting and gathering (not least in that the environment is one more or less immune to the ravages of accidental fires), the effects upon it of those involved in agriculture are likely to be far-reaching. . . . Certainly when the soil is exposed for more than two or three years by removal of the forest cover leaching occurs, levels of organic matter fall, and serious deterioration in soil fertility follows rapidly. Any form of continuous

cultivation has been (and as yet remains) impossible and the evolution of an agrarian order in the Asante forestlands has clearly involved the acquisition on the part of the cultivators, over time, of a sensitive awareness of the restraints imposed upon the exploitation of the soil by the nature of the bioclimatic system.[41]

Indeed, the dwarfs' slipperiness signifies that the ancestors' ingenuity was "magical." The vibrating masquerade, the fecundity of the "spirit presence," presents yet another commencing code.

When I asked the students about the masquerade they had encountered, the quivering mask, most of them confessed that they were unimpressed. I tried to share my appreciation of the artistry with them: the efficiency of the slight of hand, the well-crafted masquerade, the powerful subtlety of his/her dance, and the drama, the staging, of the whole event. I tried to convey to them that the humid forest-green setting and the dwarf's spirit-language reinforced his centuries-old significance. The *mmoatia* are healers as well as tricksters. They concentrate the forest's healing powers. They know its medicinal secrets and its toxicity. They are like hard-to-find roots in the dense flora. They are also master hunters. Still, most of the students said, quite literally, "That was interesting, but just give me Jesus."

Their response afflicted me with questions louder than drums: Why assume that Jesus, the very Wisdom of creation, had nothing to do with what they had experienced? Why the quick assumption that Christ nullified what they had seen? Whose hermeneutics were operating at that point? Did the students' Christology indicate the sterility I pointed out above, namely, Soyinka's observation that the upshot of universal history is that the Westernized "can only read the *spirituality* of a continent and a people in the skyline of church steeples"? Why was there no attempt to process the event in terms of the African theology I had taught them? Why no attempt to consider Kä Mana's view that many traditional religionists have concluded that the white man's religion has not brought the promised fullness of life: "Not having been received and lived as a fundamental reorientation of the essential sectors (*zones d'être*) in which posterity adjudicated life and death issues (*se décident les raisons de vivre et de mourir*), Christianity occupied an official space that traditional religionists abandoned after daring new spiritual and religious syntheses."[42]

The young medicine man, the *Sumankwafo,* had himself left the Religion to serve the forest and thus his community's autochthonous imperatives. He told us that he had attended a mission school but found that his spirit was being crushed. He thus left the church to attain the peace of mind his traditional vocation had afforded him. A rich spirituality teemed in the medicine-man's backyard. Instead of considering arguments similar to Mana's, most of the students seemed blind to another way of seeing the world made, according to John's gospel, through Jesus. Is that Christology fecund or sterile?

"This Excitement, This Discomfort"

Given the fact that the spirituality that Soyinka, the paramount, and the *Sumankwafo* uphold has been discredited by more than a century of universal history, it bears repeating that these questions are not simply christological but quite political too: Have Europe and North America allowed Africa to make the very best use of its civilizations? What contribution will African Americans, progenies of the victims of the Middle Passage, make to Africa's struggle to control its land and resources, as Baldwin has put it? To what extent has the African heritage, which Baldwin suggests involves "apprehensions, instincts, relations" of the dark gods, been "modified by the passage of time"?[43] And what do these dark gods offer with respect to the problem of "the depth and the tenacity of the great war" between black and white lifestyles in the United States? Will African Americans be so turned off by Africa's otherness, its commencing codes and neo-colonial problems, that we will "leave Africa, not to mention it again"?[44]

Chapter 7

From Ryangombe the Blood Pact to the Bloody Panga

Something is suggested of the nature of fecundity, the nature of sterility, and one realizes that it is by no means a simple matter to know which is which: the one can very easily resemble the other.   — JAMES BALDWIN[1]

Why do certain African Americans caricature Africa as an unlivable place? How does their caricature reflect the conflict between black and white lifestyles in the United States? I have found answers to some of those questions in Keith Richburg's *Out of America*, which focuses in part on the 1994 Rwandan holocaust.

Two Warring Ideals: Sterility and Fecundity

The conflict between black and white lifestyles burdened Richburg during his high school years. His *Out of America* recounts what happened after a "roller derby competition" at Detroit's Olympia Stadium. Richburg's white friends and "a group of black kids" exchanged words: "There were shouts and slurs flying in both directions." Richburg felt "trapped between two worlds" and did not want "to have to take sides." The behavior of the blacks, however, "humiliated" him. He writes: "Here's a bunch of black kids smashing the windows of [my white friends'] school bus. This is how black folks in the ghetto behaved. This is how they [the whites] would see me. I was so ashamed that I wanted to cry."[2]

The conflict of black and white lifestyles also troubled Richburg during his college years. He preferred the company of whites and so offended his black peers. Richburg claims he had failed "the dining hall test...had chosen the wrong side."[3] He wanted to resolve the question of how to be his American self among the whites he enjoyed while responding to the pressure to be a "Negro." He decided to take the *Washington Post*'s offer to cover events in Africa. "Perhaps Africa," he thought, "would reject me and my lifestyle." "Perhaps Africa would force me to choose which side of the dining hall I would sit on, and it was a choice I didn't want to make."[4]

In covering the 1994 Rwandan holocaust, Richburg watched the dead float down a river in Tanzania:

> Sometimes they came one by one. Sometimes two or three together. They were bloated now, horribly discolored. Most were naked, or stripped down to their underpants. Sometimes the hands and feet were bound together. Some were clearly missing some limbs. And as they went over the falls, a few got stuck together on a little crag, and stayed there flapping against the current, as though they were trying to break free. I couldn't take my eyes off one of them, the body of a little baby.[5]

The horrid sight makes Richburg grateful for the Middle Passage, for if his ancestor had remained in Africa, he "might have met some similarly anonymous fate in one of the countless ongoing civil wars or tribal clashes."[6] He thanks God his "ancestor got out, because, now, [he is] not one of them." Richburg thanks God he is an American.[7]

Ryangombe: Sterility or Fecundity?

Richburg blames African culture, that is, "tribalism," for the Rwandan horror because of Rwanda's precolonial history. Rwanda was comprised of the pastoral Tutsi, the agricultural Hutu, and the hunter-gatherers, the pygmy-like Twa. The tall Tutsi — the legendary, uncommonly graceful dancers who resembled "Afro-Asiatics," such as the Ethiopians or the Masai — were Rwanda's elite. The so-called Negroid Hutu of lesser stature were a Bantu people. The tiny Twa were at the bottom of the social ladder. Today such somatic distinctions between the Tutsi and the Hutu no longer hold in the same way they did in precolonial days. What is more, the Rwandan people, that is, the Banyarwandans, have never been tribal but a single people with a single culture and a single language. As Gérard Prunier put it in his book *The Rwanda Crisis: History of a Genocide,* Rwandan society "had none of the characteristics of tribes, which are micro-nations. [The Banyarwandans] shared the same Bantu language *[kinyarwanda]*, lived side by side with each other *without* any 'Hutuland' or 'Tutsiland' and often intermarried. But they were neither similar nor equal."[8] To be sure, there were tensions, but the people were not so inimical to each other that one might guess that Rwanda was bound to erupt the way that it did in 1994.

What Richburg does not consider is that Rwanda would have been livable today, would not have torn itself apart, had it retained "the coherence that existed in pre-European days."[9] Rwanda had coupled the inequality of its people with "indefinite reciprocity."[10] J. J. Maquet and Luc de Heusch both note the centrality of the Ryangombe society, an initiation society or a so-called cult, in that regard. According to de Heusch, Ryangombe suspended "caste differences between adherents."[11] According to Maquet, "The cult of Ryangombe [had] importance as a force of social cohesion. Batutsi, Bahutu and Batwa [could] all be initiated. This function [was] quite overly stressed: Ryangombe [a royal ancestor] has said himself that he should be called upon by everybody," for all have a common ancestor.[12]

The pioneering Congolese theologian Vincent Mulago also has noted the significance of Ryangombe in his essay "Le pacte du sang et la communion alimentaire: Pierres d'attente de la communion eucharistique" ("The Blood Pact and the Communion Meal: Stepping Stones to the Eucharist"). According to Mulago, Ryangombe initiates drank a powdered, sun-dried, herbal mixture of leaves and small red flowers mixed with water (*l'eau une couleur sanguinolente*) which symbolized the blood pact (*le pacte du sang*). The blood pact involved an exchange of blood called *ukunywana* (from *kunywa,* to drink): The participants imbibed a drop of each other's blood to symbolize the gift of the self merged with the Other (*fusion dans l'autre*).[13] Ryangombe thus signified the reciprocity — that is, the universality of blood — at the heart of *ukunywana.*[14] Today, however, blood symbolizes enmity in Rwanda — the virtual abolition of reciprocity. What accounts for this mutation of *le pacte du sang?*

Rwanda and the Way an Inheritance Has Been Handed Down

In *The Rwanda Crisis: History of a Genocide,* Gérard Prunier argues that the Germans, who colonized Rwanda in the late nineteenth century, and then later the Belgians, who took over from the

Germans after World War I, "were quite smitten with the Tutsi, whom they saw as definitely too fine to be 'Negroes.'"[15] Some theorists proposed that the Tutsi were the descendants of the ancient Egyptians or had come from India or Tibet. One "Belgian administrator . . . cooly speculated that the Tutsi could very well be the last survivors of the lost continent of Atlantis."[16] The whites theorized that the "winsome," "lithe" Tutsi had come from outside Rwanda to civilize the Hutu and the Twa not unlike how the Europeans had come to civilize the Africans. The imposition of a Darwinian-derived theory of racial hierarchy intensified Tutsi *hauteur* over the Hutu, who in turn cultivated an "aggressively resentful inferiority complex."[17]

In 1933–1934, the Belgians issued "'ethnic' identity cards, which labeled every Rwandan as either Hutu (eighty-five percent) or Tutsi (fourteen percent) or Twa (one percent)." The identity cards enforced the racialization of Rwanda and "the administration of an apartheid system rooted in the myth of Tutsi superiority."[18] According to Fergal Keane's *Season of Blood,* the "ID card" locked the Hutu into a permanent caste.[19] Whereas traditional life had enabled Hutu to become "Tutsified," Belgian rule made a Hutu a Hutu for life. The very land itself took on racialized meaning under European control. Prior to colonial rule, land distribution followed a well-established pattern of "inequality and reciprocity." The *Mwami* (king), for instance, did not dominate all of Rwanda, for Hutu people had retained control over choice areas, "northwest and southwest of the country."[20] Indeed, traditional struggles over land had been *"a centre versus periphery affair and not one of Tutsi versus Hutu."*[21] Under Belgian apartheid, however, "the extension and hardening of the new centralized system caused [the Hutu] to slide from a status of inferiority balanced by complementarity into that of a quasi-rural proletariat. By the end of the century the vast majority, if not the totality of the Hutu peasants, were in a position where they had to sell their labor, first as a social obligation, and then as a monetarized commodity in the colonial systems."[22]

While Richburg points out that "colonization reinforced the centuries-old ethnic and social division and laid the seeds for the upheavals that would come later," it would be more precise to argue that colonization *fabricated* the myth of "centuries-old ethnic division" — for *ethnic* division hardly existed.[23] Indeed, Richburg fails to note that an essential factor that led to the 1994 holocaust was not "tribalism" but the Roman Catholic Church in Rwanda, which promoted the Tutsi. After 1932 the church "had become [Rwanda's] main social institution, presiding over hundreds of thousands of converts, including the king himself."[24] "Catholicism...became not only linked with the highest echelons of the state but completely enmeshed in Rwandese society from top to bottom."[25] Traditional religion as embodied in Ryangombe had released social pressures exacerbated by high-density living. Roman Catholicism, however, "socially hegemonic, almost totally missing the internalized moral underpinning of Christian values, proved to be a terrible element in the violent challenge" of the traditional social structure.[26] With the church's blessing, the colonial state mercilessly taxed and conscripted the Banyarwandans, and "those who did not comply were abused and brutally beaten."[27]

According to Philip Gourevitch: "Belgium itself was a nation divided along 'ethnic' lines, in which the Francophone Wallon minority had for centuries dominated the Flemish majority. But following a long 'social revolution,' Belgium had entered an age of greater demographic equality. The Flemish priests who began to turn up in Rwanda after World War II identified with the Hutus and encouraged their aspirations for political change."[28] Flemish support expedited the church's cultivation of a counter-Hutu hegemony.

In 1959 political enmity between the Tutsi and the Hutu exploded, which escalated Belgium's support of the Hutu and hastened the 1960 elections that decided the ruling party of Rwanda — *Parmehutu*. The Tutsi, now an endangered minority, fled Rwanda in droves and organized themselves into rebel organizations. "Since late 1960, small commandos of exiled Tutsi, called *Inyenzi* (cockroaches) by the Hutu, had begun to attack from Uganda." Their attacks set off "violent reprises on the Tutsi civilian population."[29] In 1963, a year after independence, Tutsi guerillas attempted to invade Rwanda. Hutu forces crushed them and set off the first mass genocide as the Hutu government instituted a purge of *Inyenzi* (the Tutsi "insects"). Anywhere from 10,000 to 14,000 Tutsi were murdered between December 1963 and January 1964. Fergal Keane quotes Bertrand Russell as asserting that the killings constituted the "most horrible and systematic human massacre we have had occasion to witness since the extermination of the Jews by the Nazis."[30]

The 1994 genocide is perhaps the most intense holocaust of the twentieth century. Prunier points out that the word "genocide" does not pertain merely to the "magnitude of the killings" but to the fact that they were well-planned and focused on totally annihilating "targeted populations." It is not because of tribalism "that

Rwanda could suffer from a genocide; quite the contrary....In Rwanda, all the preconditions for a genocide were present: a well-organized civil service, a small tightly controlled land area, a disciplined and orderly population, reasonably good communications and a coherent ideology containing the necessary lethal potential."[31]

In concluding *Out of America,* Richburg writes:

> I'm leaving Africa now, so I don't care anymore about the turmoil in Rwanda....I've seen it all before, and I'm sure I'll see it again. But from now on, I will be seeing it from afar, maybe watching it on television like millions of other Americans....I will also know that the problems are too intractable, that the outside world can do nothing, until Africa is ready to save itself. I'll also know that none of it affects me, because I feel no attachment to the place or the people.[32]

Notwithstanding that the Rwandan genocide has more to do with European values than African ones, the genocide has helped Richburg solve his dilemma regarding "the tenacity of the great war" between black and white lifestyles. It has been solved by way of "the fabled dark continent," to make an allusion to Baldwin's *No Name in the Street.*[33] For Richburg, African sterility illumines the sterility found in the black American community. He writes that the blacks of his native Detroit have been as "tribal" as Rwanda: "The South Carolina blacks were on the west side, the Alabama blacks on the east side. And the divisions were as real as the divisions between the Hutu and Tutsi tribes in Rwanda." Alabama blacks, qua Hutus, "cuss loud in public. They don't own, they rent....They eat pigs' feet....They were in a word, 'niggers.' "[34] South Carolina blacks, qua Tutsi, were more "civilized" (but hardly as civilized as white Americans). What other than a desire to solve his "dining room" dilemma explains Richburg's strange analogy between the black America that embarrasses him and the tribal Africa that disgusts him? Recall his remark: "Perhaps Africa would force me to choose which side of the dining hall I would sit on, and it was a choice I didn't want to make." In equating Africa with barbarism — in echoing Hegel's notion that "what we properly understand by Africa is the Unhistorical, Undeveloped Spirit, still involved in the conditions of mere nature"[35] — Richburg resolves his dilemma. One can only conclude that he will never second-guess himself for preferring the company of whites.

He has resolved the "dining room" conflict through a certain obeisance: "Thank God my ancestor got out, because, now, I am not one of them."[36] Richburg has upheld Hegel's "Spirit": Africa "is no historical part of the World; it has no movement or development to exhibit."[37]

Part Four

The Mysterious
Love of God

Burning through the Veil

Chapter 8

Une surprenante analogie
Reinvesting Christian Symbols
with Their Original Energy

> The blacks did not so much use Christian symbols as rec-
> ognize them ... for what they were before the Christians
> came along — and, thus, reinvested these symbols with their
> original energy.   — JAMES BALDWIN[1]

James Baldwin has asserted that "there is a reason, after all, that
some people wish to colonize the moon, and others dance before
it as before an ancient friend."[2] For Baldwin, the distinction has to
do with Africa and America, the dark gods and the Religion, and
has apocalyptic significance: "On both continents the white and
the dark gods met in combat, and it is on the outcome of this combat that the future of both continents depends."[3] Baldwin suggests
to me that African Americans must understand the reason for the
"moon dance" to equip ourselves to withstand the sterility of the
Religion.

For Baldwin, this sterility involves the fact that "the Christian
church has betrayed and dishonored and blasphemed that Saviour
in whose name they have slaughtered millions and millions and
millions of people."[4] According to Baldwin, this betrayal of the
gospel has been due to "the total hardening of the heart and the
coarsening of the conscience among those people who believed
that their power has given them the exclusive right to history."[5]
Baldwin has posed a discomforting question in the light of this history: "If the Christians do not believe in their Saviour (who has
certainly, furthermore, failed to save them) why, then, wonder the
unredeemed, should I abandon my gods for yours?"[6] Witnessing
to his threshing floor experience, Baldwin asserts the fecundity of
his spirituality: "I *know* my gods are real: they have enabled me
to withstand you [i.e., the white gods of the Religion]."[7] Surely the

pangolin's royal armor, the *mmoatia*'s green magic, and Rwanda's *Ukunywana* suggest why: They empower blacks to define themselves and respect their ancestors. There is indeed a reason why people have danced before the moon.

Recognizing Christian Symbols before the Christians Came Along

Would Rwanda have torn itself apart if it had appropriated the gospels free from the Religion partly responsible for the 1994 holocaust? Sigmund Freud's postmodern psychology posits that "the aim of all life is death" — that life is wired to actualize its "inanimate" beginnings.[8] Freud claims that life has evolved because a "civilizing" drive restrains the powerful striving to fulfill "the final aim of life as swiftly as possible." Freud's argument is not unlike Hegel's "*cunning...reason* that...sets the passions to work for itself, while that which develops its existence through such impulsion pays the penalty, and suffers loss."[9] In both cases, the *extinction* of human life is deemed as necessary for the attainment of the universal.

I believe, however, that Levinas's anthropology is closer to the fecundity I am after — to Baldwin's sense of the reason for the moon dance. It is that anthropology that compels me to doubt that Rwanda would have torn itself asunder. Recall that for Levinas, the foundation of spirituality and ethics is the "denucleating" responsibility to give the Other the bread out of one's mouth — a responsibility that is more "structural" than the impulse to violate the Other. For Levinas, then, no death instinct stands "behind the I, unknown to the conscious I...fettering it anew."[10] So whereas Freud holds that even fecundity, construed as human sexuality, signifies sterility, the death instinct, "a need to restore an earlier state of things," Levinas holds that "fecundity evinces a unity that is not opposed to multiplicity, but, in the precise sense of the term, engenders it."[11] For Levinas, the human race is *free* to promote a proliferating diversity; for Freud, the human race is *bound* to a cosmic sterility. For Levinas, the responsibility for the Other is the maternal fecundity from which we spring — "the preoriginal signifyingness that gives sense, because it gives."[12]

Vincent Mulago makes a similar point: Unity, the "telos" of life, is not actualized through the dog-eat-dog instinct for cold, mute totality. Unity is actualized through the "denucleating," live-and-let-live spirituality that strives for diversity. In the Ryangombe society, the blood pact, representing fecundity, was more than a symbol of one's self. It was "a part of me, a part of my self" — *principe vital*.[13] This gift of the self is neither a racial nor a clannish gift, but courses toward the vast horizons that expand and enlarge the meaning of the human family.[14] Such fecundity involved not only blood but the communal meal as well. People ate from the same plate and sipped from the same straw (*chalumeau*). The meal thus signified a vital unity that flowed through the community.[15] By way of Ryangombe, then, Tutsi, Hutu, and Twa had begun to cultivate God's mysterious love — "vast horizons that expand and enlarge the meaning of the human family" — before the Euro-missionaries came.

For Mulago, African culture offers the gospel fertile ground in which to grow. Holy communion, for example — *symbole des symboles, le Sacrement des sacrements* — can put down roots in Ryangombe's quest to fuse with the neighbor and the dead (*le monde suprasensible*). In that sense, Mulago's spirituality incorporates rather than nullifies the victims of universal history. Hegel is significantly different. He claims that Africans' ancestor veneration is a small step from magic. Although he recognizes that the veneration of ancestors has "the character of something more universal, something elevated to thought" — in that Africans realized a "form of representation" that "is not in the immediate present" — he concludes that the African dead are no stepping stones to genuine transcendence as they are tied to the crisis of the moment — flood, famine, volcano — and propitiated accordingly: "Present . . . effects are to some extent attributed to them, and a remedy for these ills is sought from them."[16]

According to Hegel, the Africans are still enslaved to the irrational because they believe that their ancestors cause both fortune and misfortune: "What we call 'natural' these people still do not yet know to be natural."[17] In his book *The Philosophy of History*, Hegel points out: "In Negro life the characteristic point is the fact that consciousness has not yet attained to the realization of any substantial objective existence — as for example, God, or Law — in which the interest of man's volition is involved and in which he realizes his own being."[18] Mulago, however, approaches the situation differently. The Africans, the Banyarwandans in this case, had a concept of God (*Imana*), though they did not know he had a Son, whose Spirit embraces all people without nullifying their autochthonous (i.e., created) wisdom.

V. Y. Mudimbe points out that Mulago's *African* theology is a viable strategy "for technically reconciling such competing theses as outsiders' models and insiders' paradigms and expectations." The theology itself, though, is *weighted* in a synthesis of Enlightenment-influenced anthropology and Roman Catholic dogmatics.[19] According to Mudimbe, then, Mulago's work, especially his essay *"Le pacte du sang et communion alimentaire,"* "claims to unveil the uncontaminated fundamentals and proprieties of regional localities [such as Rwanda], yet it is not in their own specificities, nor in the experience of their traditions and the intentional acts of past explicit actors, but rather from their possible grasp, understanding and sublimation by Christianity."[20] According to Mudimbe, Mulago thus "comments on the failure of 'traditional intellectuals,' and transcends ancient canons using the authority of new forms of consciousness."[21] But this move involves a contradiction: Mulago uses the problematized ancestral wisdom to indigenize the alien forms.[22]

Mudimbe recognizes, however, that "important divergences and sometimes conflicting choices existed between the policies of colonial powers and those of Christian missions."[23] However nominally, Christians have advanced progressive and liberating causes in the Religion's colonial space. What is more, Mudimbe argues that

> Christianity was advancing in a fertile terrain. Local beliefs about life and death, destiny and history conveyed ideas about a transcendent divinity and superior spirits. Moreover, throughout the continent mythological charters had been transmitting for centuries narratives on the creation of the earth, the original sin, universal flood, etc., all of them perfectly reconcilable with biblical lessons. Other lines of coincidence, particularly such ritual practices as circumcision, regular prayers to God(s), celebration and veneration of ancestors, should also be added.[24]

In short, an African Christian, making much of Baldwin's reason, could well argue that God's Wisdom had not abandoned Africa, that Africa's sense of "transcendent divinity and superior spirits" complemented biblical themes more so than the white man's religion.

In effect, Ryangombe and the blood pact, however much an example of what Mudimbe calls "retrodiction," *would* have been far more appropriate for the Africanization of the gospel than the Religion that dominated ecclesial politics in Rwanda. According to Mudimbe:

> Retrodiction — from Latin *retro* (on the back side, behind, in time back) and *dicere* (to speak) — denotes the idea of speaking (and thus synthesizing) from an illusory, invented moment back in time. In the process, the present invests its values in the past with its questions and hypotheses, and rediscovers in the invented, reorganized spaces, laws, paradigms, or the truth of its suppositions... often in contradiction with the colonial adapted Enlightenment paradigms and its library.[25]

From that library's perspective, *le pacte du sang* — understood perhaps as a sublimated mode of anthropophagy — was all too heathen. Yet Mulago claims that the blood pact anticipates "the communicant's individual union with Christ: 'He who eats my flesh and drinks my blood abides in me, and I in him.' Thanks to that immanence, the Eucharist establishes between Christ and his disciples a vital exchange, a flow of one life into another life: 'As the living Father sent me, and I live because of the Father, so he who eats me will live because of me' [John 6:57]."[26] A gospel truth asserts itself here: Jesus' disciples misconstrue his words as some mystical appeal to anthropophagy — "a hard saying, who can listen to it?" (John 6:60). This saying is so difficult that "many of his disciples no longer went about with him" (John 6:66).

According to Mulago, a *Manyarwandan,* a Rwandan, probably would not have been scandalized by the hard saying. He or she likely would have understood the Christ, for cannibalism is inconceivable in that traditional society. The blood pact thus equipped Banyarwandans to catch the import of God's mysterious love: to partake of the Other's blood is not to destroy him or her but to give him or her time and space for abundant life.[27] For Mulago, Ryangombe invests the sacrament with an *original energy:* flesh and blood and its alimentary symbols compellingly complement the Last Supper. Gathered up into the crucified God, *le pacte du sang* (the blood pact), though unwise in today's AIDS-ridden Africa, anticipated a certain perichoresis. The one is *in* the other. Tutsi, Hutu, and Twa are three and one.

For Mulago, then, Holy Communion hardly serves to nullify the "*participation-communion alimentaire* and the blood pact of our Bantu." That Mulago writes "our Bantu" (*nos Bantou*) is ironic in that he is implying that the blood pact is a Hutu imperative: Their role in the holocaust is thus a tragic transmo-grification indeed. An astonishing analogy (*surprenante analogie*) constitutes the two modalities, the Christian sacrament and Ryan-gombe. "Through and through, though the two modes are most distinct, each signifies a profound sociality: there is *incorpora-tion, participation-communion* — the communion of all life at the boundary of the other, a penetration into his or her being, per-mitting and realizing an exchange — life flowing from one to the other."[28]

Mulago's humane, if "neo-colonial," efforts raise once more the theologically compelling question: Would Rwanda have torn itself apart if it had appropriated the gospels free from the Reli-gion partly responsible for the 1994 holocaust? Assuredly, Mulago provides one with a Christian substantiation of Baldwin's claim that people moon-dance for a *good* reason. The fact that what Soyinka has called slave ontology carries the opprobrium of that reason "on the brow" notwithstanding, *because of* Christian iden-tity as Mudimbe and Baldwin have pointed out, the positive re-evaluation of that reason is integral to an Africana spirituality that is ambivalently Christian today.

The Free Choice for the Other

Perhaps no one is a more engrossing figure for an Africana spir-ituality in the Christian fold than the late Engelbert Mveng: négritude poet, Pan-Africanist, head of the Ecumenical Association of African Theologians, and Jesuit priest. In 1995 assassins mur-dered Mveng for his condemnation of human rights violations in his native Cameroon. They dismembered him in his home. Father Mveng began his public service career as director of the *Service des affaires culturelles,* a division of Cameroon's Ministry of Ed-ucation, a position in which he helped inventory "the country's museum artifacts, library holdings, archival resources and artisanal capacities."[29] Mveng believed that traditional, as in "precolonial," spirituality — moon dance if you will — was an inner vitality that would liberate his people from the racist values of French colonial-ism. Without question, that precolonial, or rather invented, culture had to be baptized for the Mveng of the early 1970s: "He saw Cameroonian identity in terms of an evolution that commenced in the authentic traditions of a precolonial past and was moving toward a new unity based on the synthesis of African values and Christian ideals."[30]

Mveng's *Black African Art: Cosmic Liturgy and Religious Language,* (1974), a seminal work in African theology, illustrates that synthesis. Mveng's premise is that God's mysterious love sustains a traditional Bantu spirituality that is coded in artifacts and other religious modes such as polyrhythm and prayer. According to Mveng, moreover, traditional Bantu prayer bears an affinity to the Bible in that both signify a three-dimensional spirituality that entails a vision of the world, a vision of humankind and humility before God.[31] Those complementary relations — world, humankind, God — are united "thanks to the dialectical axis" of *participation universelle.* God, who affirms himself in creation "ineluctably" as a transcendent, radical alterity, is the source of this universal participation.[32]

For Mveng, humans' consciousness of *participation universelle* is the image of God. Humankind alone, then, knows what is of God and what is anti-God. The following premise is thus at the very heart of Mveng's apocalyptic argument: Only human beings know that the world is comprised of Adversaries and Allies and thus aligned in two camps — that of Life on the one side and Death on the other.[33] According to Mveng, Africans perceive the world's twoness as a cosmic drama, a struggle — the meaning of which is the triumph of freedom over determinism (perceived as adversarial). Traditional Bantu prayer voices that hope, that dogged strength, as it trusts that God has been in solidarity with the human struggle for fecundity despite the sterility that accompanies life. When faced with the ostensible triumph of that sterility, the African, with much fury and anguish, prayed, "Oh God help us to live."[34]

Black African prayer is thus the *verbe salvifique* as it refuses capitulation to death's negation of life. Even magico-religious practices indicate what is at issue, for who but God's image can "make" the cosmos fecund? For Mveng, however, magic (consider the *mmoatia* of chapter six) means that traditional angst had not yet burned through the veils of a cosmos set against itself. To put that another way: Practices related to magic constitute the moribund echo of primal, naked prayer. For Mveng, then, when pangolin sacrifice failed to promote cosmic equilibrium, Africans turned to the one God, the Other, the Source of Life.

Mveng thus argues that black Africans' prayers signify "the call of a perpetually new life, and a constant 'yes' to the coming

life. The first thing that strikes one in that regard is the character of Bantu prayer turned-toward-the-future. One prays for the
new moon, for the new day, for the descending night, for the new
seasons.... Prayer is thus properly speaking an *initiation* in the et-
ymological sense of the word.... It is 'yes' to the coming life."[35]
From that perspective, then, the *mmoatia* and the royal pangolin
represent a dogged strength, God-given, within the cosmic veil.
The human being tries mightily to subdue sterility and so reads
on the world's face the name of his or her allies — the antelope,
the pangolin, and so on. Burning through those modalities when
the chips are down, the African calls on God when finite freedom
fails. Prayer, as cosmic language, reflects the hominized call of a
menaced life.[36]

This cosmic language is coded in African artifacts. Mveng points
out Baluba (Congo) and Dogon (Mali) initiation masks, the crests
of which bear an encircled cross. Here, the extremities of the
world, its circumference, are signified by the four roads — North,
South, East, and West — which converge at the center point of
the cross. The convergence of the four directions signifies the in-
tersection of life and death.[37] For Mveng, the initiation masks
have anticipated the comprehensiveness of Christ's cross and the
life-and-death implications of its crossroads structure. The cross
(*l'arbre du cosmos*), by virtue of *le sauveur qui y pend* (i.e., the cru-
cifix), is "the mystery of life." For here, God and humankind are
truly one; and the meaning of this "perfect encounter" is that death
only temporarily negates God's mysterious love, God's gift of life.
The Christian cross thus completes the African cross in confirming
Africans' cosmic insights regarding the victory of life over death.[38]

As Mveng sees it, then, the resurrection from the dead hardly
negates the traditional wisdom of the elders who presided over the
rites of initiation. Initiation involved a descent to a certain threshing floor, a terrible fall. There in the void likened to death, the
ancestors harshly but edifyingly taught the enduring lessons of a
fecund humanity. According to Mveng, posterity has recorded one
such lesson: Masked guides taught young initiates that human beings had long ago lamented the inevitability of death and asked
God to deliver them from it. Why must death devour us? God said
in reply, "You don't know what it is to *live*. Go. Teach your sons
that without death there is no life."[39] The commitment to precar-
ious life is especially symbolized by the moon: "The new moon is
the Pan-African symbol. Ancestral wisdom has said that the new
moon is like an evil eye: She can bring misfortune and therefore

signals a critical phase of the struggle for life. When the moon rose in pre-colonial days, black Africa was praying."[40] (And dancing, Baldwin suggests.) In short, the masked guides' lesson comple- ments a gospel truth: life overcomes death; life is the salvific and ultimate word. The new moon symbolizes this truth in that its waning (death) is tied to its waxing (life). The inevitability of the former state means that each new cycle proffers death, from which God alone, as the gospel indicates, rescues one.

According to Mveng, African art focuses on life in the stark- est of signs (namely, *les organes physique de la génération*, that is, the sexual organs). Mveng argues that this "sacramental" di- mension signifies the commitment to fecundity. Sexuality as symbol thus sings the victory of life as exigency and as archetype, but only in the sense that the struggle for life is dogged, perpetual.[41] For Mveng, the Bantu struggle against the Adversary, sterility, lifts up sexuality as the movement from the *monade* to the *dyade*, and then to the fecund principle itself: the *triade*, new life. The *monade — donnée objective*, condemned to indetermination — is masculinity; the *dyade* is femininity, which presupposes its male counterpart; and the *triade* is the synthesis: "the victory of life under the sign of fecundity."[42] For Mveng, this threefold structure is the a priori of all ethics. The ethical commences when human beings assume this threefold structure and fructifies it in opting for freedom and re- sponsibility, thereby becoming persons.[43] In choosing to make the best of the *dyade*, in choosing to be social, in choosing to promote life, humankind becomes free, responsible, and personal.[44]

As seen in its initiation societies, Africa's sense of personal responsibility is strong. According to Mveng, initiation is the memory of the primordial choice for freedom — responsibility as male and female. This free choice for the Other, constitutive of human personality, renders humankind both free and loving. As free and loving, "man-woman" moves toward the third moment and "actualizes" the imago Dei and passes from male-female being to become father-mother-child, the triumph of life — fecundity.[45] Mveng's point is that a Bantu has always seen him- or herself as a crowd. It is thus "impossible to separate the intrinsic social and in- dividual dimensions."[46] African art therefore sings the memory of the roads taken toward human realization. Mveng thus takes the pulse of his anthropology in the movement from the *dyade* to the *triade*. The wave of the duration, as represented in African drum- ming and dance, thus signifies that humanized time "is not a sum of identical instants that succeed each other, but a totalization in

the present of all that the past has become in growing in us."[47]
At the same time, rhythm, movement, signifies that the future —
life! — is always sustaining us.[48]

Singing the Victory of Life on the Hither Side of the Master-Slave Dialectic

If the missionaries violated the mysterious love of God by dismem-
bering the art and prayer Mveng champions, then his work, and
Mulago's, has indeed invested Christian symbols with their original energy. If African spirituality as construed in Africana terms
has embodied a future-bound commitment to fecund life, why
would that spirituality have to be colonized to be Christian unless
the Religion has, à la Freud, served sterile ends? Mveng has argued compellingly that a people need not have been Europeanized
to recognize Jesus' cosmic cross. Managing two warring ideals,
a "pagan" sensibility and a high Christology, Mveng's "dogged
strength alone" enabled him to burn through colonial hubris with
a compelling, but one-sided, hermeneutic.

According to Mveng, the Hegelian master-slave (*maître-esclave*)
dialectic was the animus behind colonial rule. Mveng holds that the

> master-slave dialectic is not structural to African thought and
> constitutes no a priori moment of our symbolic vision of the
> world. We surely cannot ignore that dialectic, but we situ-
> ate it in history, at the level of the deeds produced by free
> persons. It is incontestable that Marx's social dialectic has
> profoundly marked the West and that the battle between mas-
> ter and slave, exemplified first of all in class struggle, has
> become a general axiom of the modern West. But for we
> blacks, the relations of man-nature and man-man give way
> to a threefold dialectic because it is essentially grounded in
> the biological unity of the world. Thus the male and female
> relation bears fruit in the *triade* Father-Mother-Child.[49]

For Mveng, then, the "biological unity of the world" precedes the
misuse of human freedom. That unity is a prehistoric value deeply
etched in African spirituality.

According to Mveng, however, slavery and colonialism have de-
formed African spirituality. He writes: "Paganism, above all where
slavery or colonialism has inflicted havoc on the foundations of the

psyche, knows the phenomenon of 'possession': possession by the spirits or forces of nature rather than ecstasy in God. It is easy to see that authentic conversion eliminates in one stroke the causes of this phenomenon."[50] For Mveng, then, African Christians in the independent churches, which encourage such behavior, undermine both African spirituality and Christian truth. In sum, Mveng attributes possession trance to Westernization, whites' imposition of universal history onto Africa, and construes possession trance as an abnormality of African religion, which marks the violence of Western invasion. Mveng, however, makes no mention of the slavery indigenous to Africa. That was not his focus, and one cannot cover all things, but it should be noted that the Bamoun people of his native Cameroon, who, according to Mveng, exemplify the spirituality of African art so preeminently, apparently thrived on slavery.

According to Claude Meillassoux's book *The Anthropology of Slavery: The Womb of Iron and Gold*, "two-thirds of the population was enslaved in the Bamoum [i.e,, Bamoun] kingdom."[51] The economy was dependent on slaves to work the fields and thus provide the necessary food source.[52] The entire kingdom took part in the raids that procured slaves.[53]

Given Mveng's theological commitments, perhaps his intent has been simply to uphold the values that hail from what Meillassoux calls "domestic non-slave society," which preceded African slavery and was the victim of it. Consistent with Mveng's perspective — that is, that "the master-slave dialectic is not central to African thought and constitutes no a priori moment of our symbolic vision of the world" — domestic non-slave society *balanced* the reproductive and productive cycles and assimilated *aliens* into the kinship matrix. Indeed, Meillassoux argues that Bamoun slavery, "to the extent that we have defined it as reproducing itself through capture, seems to have dominated relations of production at court and among the aristocracy."[54] An "indeterminate proportion of agricultural laborers were allotment or settled slaves," however; though their "social status was inferior," they "were permitted to live in a couple and to have progeny. It does not seem that any kind of 'patriarchal slavery' developed among ordinary people."[55] Perhaps, then, Mveng's assertion that black Africa eschewed the master-slave dialectic in favor of the father-mother-child dialectic reflects a peasant's ancient sensibility.

For Mveng the master-slave dialectic rather than the father-mother-child dialectic is behind Africa's current dysfunction. The former dialectic divides the world into two camps: "Something is suggested of the nature of fecundity, the nature of sterility, and one realizes that it is by no means a simple matter to know which is which: the one can very easily resemble the other." For Mveng, the master's form, which Morrison countered through the antelope dance, and which plunged Baldwin down to his very pagan roots and forced Du Bois to the Ghanian soil that enshrines him, is the problem of evil.[56] Mveng thought that Africa's humane wisdom might help it overcome the legacy of slavery and colonialism. Tragically, assassins brutally murdered Mveng because he sought human rights for all. He is a casualty of neo-colonial Africa, which forgets all too often why its peasants danced before the moon.

Chapter 9

The Mysterious Love
of a Third-Party God

Fury and anguish filled [John Grimes], unbearable, unanswerable; his mind was stretched to breaking. For it was *time* that filled his mind, *time* that was violent *with the mysterious love of God.* And his mind could not contain the terrible stretch of *time* that united twelve men fishing by the shores of Galilee, and black men weeping on their knees tonight, and he, a witness. . . . There was an awful silence at the bottom of John's mind, a dreadful weight, a dreadful speculation. And not even speculation, but a deep, deep turning, as of something huge, black, shapeless, for ages dead on the ocean floor, that now felt its rest disturbed by a faint, far wind, which bid it: "Arise." And this weight began to move at the bottom of John's mind, in a silence like the silence of the void before creation, and he began to feel a terror he had never felt before.

— JAMES BALDWIN[1]

"The mysterious love of God" is a theme from James Baldwin's *Go Tell It on the Mountain:* In his dusty storefront Harlem church, John Grimes found himself angst-ridden one Saturday night. "The terrible stretch of time" — which united the first century's gospels to the weeping black folk, the victims of the Middle Passage — set John on edge. *Time violent with the mysterious love of God* made him think of some drowned leviathan that had been "for ages dead on the ocean floor." The weight of that history, itself the burden of what Soyinka has called "slave ontology," moved "at the bottom of John's mind, in a silence like the silence of the void before creation, and he began to feel a terror he had never felt before." He panicked because a dreadful speculation unnerved him: If God could not make sense of his shrouded existence because God had

anchored him to the "ocean floor," then God would be nothing
but the master and the dusty saints but slaves to the form of God.

Time Violent with the Mysterious
Love of God

Later, as he was well along in practicing his vocation as a writer,
Baldwin realized that he had thrashed on the church's floor because
the huge something below him was inseparable from the mystery
of God's eternal love above him. The gospel stories of disciples
"fishing by the shores of Galilee" had been real to Baldwin precisely because he realized that the legacy of the Middle Passage
had placed him close to Jesus Christ, the incarnate love of God.
That is, the "pagan desperation" that gave him some relief from
the white god has a certain christological significance. As Baldwin
put it in an essay he penned for the *Ecumenical Review* entitled
"White Racism or World Community," he considered himself "one
of God's creatures" who brought to life "a plea...articulated by
Jesus Christ himself, who said, 'Insofar as you have done it to the
least of these, you have done it all to me.' "[2] His appeal to Matthew
25:40 complements certain well-known Christologies, themselves
opposed to the sterility, the nothingness, of the Religion, from
which God's mysterious love lifts "the least of these."

Dietrich Bonhoeffer's *Creation and Fall,* for instance, which
marks his increasing opposition to the Nazis, provides a basis for
the view that the gospel reveals that the cross and the resurrection
signify a certain sterility and a certain fecundity: a nothingness and
a *mysterion.* As the issue of a too-small concept of God, the crucifixion is sterility, the godless embrace of the nothingness that is
overcome by the Creator's love. In raising Jesus from that sterility, "the silence of the void before creation," as Baldwin put it,
God's fecundity overflows as a mysterious love for mortal life — "a
means of liberation and not a means to control others."[3] For Bonhoeffer, this liberation means that God raises up the new creation
in "the form of a servant."[4] For Bonhoeffer, then, the future is the
resurrection *from* the dead — the Creator's glorified, anhypostatic
humanity, "the new creation."[5] God's fecundity thus rises from
sterility, a point Bonhoeffer makes in opposition to Hegel's philosophy, which, Bonhoeffer claims, enthrones reason "in the place
of God."[6] For Bonhoeffer, such reason is self-glorifying.[7]

For Jürgen Moltmann, the cross means that God suffers the death of his Son. God becomes "smaller," so to speak — a mortality (qua death in God), which corresponds to Moltmann's appropriation of the Lurian notion of *zinsum*. According to Isaac Luria, God, having been most infinitely and eternally alone, makes room for what-is-not-God. This divine *contraction* is the precondition for "the silence of the void before creation." Creation out of nothing thus denotes the absence of God as God contracts, becomes smaller, until there is in part no-God. Yet that sterility, that is, no-God — for "the *nihil* in which God creates his creation is God-foresakenness, hell, absolute death" — is the "ground" of fecundity:[8] "That space [qua] void does not become 'empty space' because of...withdrawal." It is rather "qualified and structured through the God who receives...creation."[9] God received creation's fury and anguish through the crucifixion of the Beloved Son (Mark 15:34). His death is the sterility through which the eternal God is in solidarity with mortified humanity and indeed the totality of transient creation.

For Bonhoeffer and Moltmann, therefore, God's form is not that of the master but that of the Risen Jew, who was crucified as a slave. God is thus inseparable from what the master would crucify (nullify). Baldwin was not in the process of falling away from *God,* who is "otherwise than being" (Levinas), otherwise than the master's form, but was in the process of realizing his solidarity with Jesus' God (Matt 25:31–37).

The Mysterious Love of God and Third-Person Christology (Father/Spirit/Son)

If Baldwin has identified the American side of this experience of Jesus' God, the late Engelbert Mveng has identified its Pan-African implications in terms of *pauvreté anthropologique,* that is, anthropological wretchedness. This slave ontology negates the fundamental rights, cultures, religions, and institutions of African people. The upshot of such wretchedness is that black people have believed that they have no right to live, love, hope, and this assault on their spirituality is, according to Mveng, part of a vast conspiracy of those who have exploited Africa and oppressed its Diaspora.[10]

Father Mveng derived his concept of anthropological wretchedness from the Beatitudes, themselves introduced by an unforget-
table litany of wretchedness (Matt 4:24ff.). Here the Spirit calls
one to see the faces of those the master claims have no right to
exist (Matt 5:3), and no right to love (Matt 5:11), and no right
to hope (Matt 5:6). Mveng was thus edified by the spirituality of
the Beatitudes, which was for him the spirituality of liberation. He
writes: "The Gospel favors the poor, the weak, the oppressed, but
is not about the poor and oppressed seizing power. The Kingdom
the Beatitudes announce is theirs, but it is, moreover, God's Kingdom, that of heaven [the future], which is the Kingdom of justice,
peace, love: the ultimate liberation."[11]

In asserting that the gospel is not about the poor seizing power
but is about God's kingdom — that is, Christ himself, who had
been the most wretched of all — Mveng provides one with another
nuance of *pauvreté anthropologique*. Mveng argues that *pauvreté
anthropologique* also signifies the spiritual vacuity of those who
have seized power as if they were the upholders of God's kingdom. For Mveng, then, anthropological wretchedness can take on
"theological," that is, theistic, forms as "it drains, voids, persons
of everything that can enable them to recognize Christ as a person" (Matt 25:40).[12] This anthropological wretchedness enthrones
the master in the place of Christ. Here, the "masters of Western
theology ... have monopolized Christ, the church, the faith, and the
world, and ... claim that their discourse is universal theology."[13]

Ludwig Feuerbach, in contrast to Hegel, suggests that the master's universal theology "confesses, what in reflection on itself,
as theology, it will not admit; namely, that God is an altogether
human being" — the master, for my purposes.[14] For Feuerbach,
then, the incarnation is "no mysterious composition of contraries,
no synthetic fact," no *communicatio idiomatum* or hypostatic
union, but a means by which "the subjective man [i.e., the form
of God] makes his feelings the measure, the standard, of what
ought to be. That which does not please him, which offends his
transcendental, supranatural, or antinatural feelings, ought not to
be." According to Feuerbach, a certain Mariology exemplifies such
nullification. The "wearisome laws of logic and physics" notwithstanding — the self is "pleased with the idea of the Mother, but
only of the Mother who already carries the infant on her arms."[15]
A fortiori, Mary's virginity and the two-natures Christology that
upholds it would serve to insulate the metaphysical Subject, the
Son, from what James Baldwin has called "the stink of life." The

sterilization of conception is thus an escape from history. As Feuerbach points out: "Only because the God-man was not infected with
original sin, could he, the pure one, purify mankind in the eyes
of God, to whom the natural process of generation was an object
of aversion, *because he himself is nothing else but supranatural
feeling.*"[16]

Squeamish in the face of the misery Mark's Jesus handles with
spit and compassion, *supranatural feeling* is prone to throw a deaf
ear to the injustice that undermines fecundity for *all*. Hence the
form of God, Hegel's "World-Historical Individual," is impervi-
ous to the third person's fury and anguish, his or her *pauvreté
anthropologique*. Here the form of God might well consider Feuerbach's questions — "Who is our Saviour and Redeemer? God or
Love?" — without subscribing to Feuerbach's atheism, which Moltmann calls "anthropotheism."[17] A god who is but the Western self
is, as Mveng and Baldwin suggest, a loveless master blind to, and
moreover terrified of, the promise that "Love" is "our Saviour."
"For God as God has not saved us, but Love, which transcends
the difference between the divine and human personality."[18] If we
"sacrifice love to God," as we do in service to the form of God,
"we have the God — the evil being — of religious fanaticism."[19]

Mveng suggests, however, that the God of the Beatitudes does
not signify theistic alienation, how we experience God. Rather, the
Beatitudes signify how God experiences us — that God, the Creator of heaven and earth, is in mysterious, perichoretic solidarity
with the third person: the Son who dies as a slave. If that is so,
then God is no master but a fellow sufferer, whose pain is peri-
choretically reflected in the dying Jesus and the future of the Spirit's
third-person way in the world. Love, then, mysterious love, is discovered in proximity to *pauvreté anthropologique,* especially that
of the slave rather than that of the master. How imperative to
know which is which!

If the crucified Jesus is "light of light," then the gospel draws
our attention to a fecund *pauvreté anthropologique* in God, a
fellow-sufferer with the crucified Son, who comes to mind in the
end time through Baby Suggs's torn-asunderness. The mysterious
love of God thus "lays hold of us and other people at the point
where we are finished, and give up. The location of [the mysterious
love of God]...is the misery of despair, and the blatant injustice
which makes us despair; for where else should it display its creative power, the power which raises up, and puts things to rights?
Where else can it manifest itself except in whatever says 'no' to

life? [The setting in life] of creative love is death."[20] It is in that sense, in the sense of God's loss of the Beloved Son, that the gospel stretches out to us from the future. The One who had been dead awaits us as the mystery of an indestructible love. The future is thus flesh of our flesh and blood of our blood, the future a hateful Religion tries to destroy.

Let the Dreams of the Dead Rebuke the Blind

Throughout this book, I have placed this future in proximity to Africa's and America's *pauvreté anthropologique,* which calls one to responsibility for the traces of the ancestors in Africana spirituality today: the *Tyiwara,* the *mmoatia,* the pangolin, Ryangombe. Here a nullified humanity calls to mind God's justice for all third persons. This God is vast and has absorbed and diachronically will raise all of humankind through the Spirit. One day (and it won't be long) all will see that God is *not* the apotheosis of our manifold bigotries, which demand that certain pasts remain forever dead. Du Bois put it this way (he was but five years shy of having lived for a hundred years and knew that he would soon join the invisible deep within the veil): "Let...the Dreams of the Dead rebuke the Blind who think that what is will be forever and teach them that what was worth living for must live again and that which merited death must stay dead. Teach us, Forever Dead, there is no Dream but Deed, there is no Deed but Memory."[21]

I, for one, remember Du Bois. I will always cherish that time I spent at his grave in Ghana. Near the slave castles that launched the Middle Passage, I meditated on his dreams and took his deeds, his dogged strength, his courage, to heart. I also remember the antelope dancers Toni Morrison unveils in *Beloved.* I imagine their faces (saltwater folk "stooping in a watery field").[22] I remember Baldwin's witness too: "The questions which one asks oneself begin, at last, to illuminate the world, and become one's key to the experience of others. One can only face in others what one can face in oneself. On this confrontation depends the measure of our wisdom and compassion. This energy is all that one finds in the rubble of vanished civilizations, and the only hope for ours."[23]

Throughout this book, my contention has been that the gospel is not identical with the Religion, upholder that it has been of a frustrating double standard. And so a dogged strength, emergent from the upward path of Du Bois's double-consciousness, has burned through the shrouding activity of the Religion and discovered that the mysterious love of God embodies the inner strength that resists injustice — an inside vitality that, aided by insight into one's virtue and one's oppressors' vices, empowers one to reject a nullifying double standard — for the dead and the living and the unborn. "The mysterious love of God" thus signifies a spirituality that comes *from* God who is loved *in* a certain Africana consciousness, the love of the black body, as it were. All that I have had to say about spirituality has been inseparable from a long history that afflicts my body with an opprobrium wed to the global problem of the Same — an unjust aesthetic, a noetic pretentiousness — through which I have burned, from which I am free for ever and ever. The nullifying form of "God" is not *my* Creator. High-priced coercion is no *conversion* at all. I am so very grateful for the dogged strength to say so within the veil.

Notes

Chapter 1: "Ever at Thy Glowing Altar": The Problem

1. Countee Cullen, "Heritage," in *The Book of Negro Poetry* (ed. James Weldon Johnson; New York: Harcourt, Brace, and World, 1958), 224.

2. Winthrop Jordan, *White over Black: American Attitudes toward the Negro, 1550–1812* (New York: W. W. Norton, 1977), 210–12.

3. William Jones, *Is God a White Racist? A Preamble to Black Theology* (Boston: Beacon Press, 1998), xv.

4. Ibid., 210.

5. Ibid., xv.

6. Anthony Pinn, *Why Lord? Suffering and Evil in Black Theology* (New York: Continuum, 1995), 157.

7. Ibid., 157.

8. Victor Anderson, *Beyond Ontological Blackness: An Essay on African American Religious and Cultural Criticism* (New York: Continuum, 1995), 120.

9. Ibid., 87.

10. Ibid.

11. Toni Morrison, *Playing in the Dark: Whiteness and the Literary Imagination* (Cambridge: Harvard University Press, 1992), 50; emphasis added.

12. Ibid., 65.

13. Ibid.

14. James Baldwin, "Everybody's Protest Novel," in *Notes of a Native Son* (Boston: Beacon Press, 1984), 21.

15. Lewis R. Gordon, *Bad Faith and Antiblack Racism* (Atlantic Highlands, N.J.: Humanities Press, 1995), 148.

16. W. E. B. Du Bois, *Dusk of Dawn: An Essay toward an Autobiography of a Race Concept* (New Brunswick, N.J.: Transaction Books 1984), 170.

17. Ibid., 157.

18. W. E. B. Du Bois, *Darkwater: Voices from within the Veil* (Millwood, N.Y.: Kraus-Thompson, 1975), 36.

19. Pinn, *Why Lord?*, 157.

20. W. E. B. Du Bois, *The Autobiography of W. E. B. Du Bois: A Soliloquy on Viewing My Life from the Last Decade of Its First Century* (New York: International Publishers, 1991), 410.

21. Jones, *Is God a White Racist?* 195.

22. Ibid.

23. Jürgen Moltmann, *The Crucified God: The Cross as the Foundation and Criticism of Christian Theology* (Minneapolis: Fortress Press, 1993), 68.

24. Jürgen Moltmann, "Introduction," *Union Seminary Quarterly Review* 31, no. 1 (fall 1975): 4.

25. W. E. B. Du Bois, *The Souls of Black Folk* (New York: Alfred A. Knopf, 1993), 16.

26. Moltmann, "Introduction," 4.

27. Georg Wilhelm Friedrich Hegel, *The Philosophy of History* (New York: Dover, 1956), 49.

28. Ibid., 99.

29. Ibid., 98.

30. V. Y. Mudimbe, *The Invention of Africa: Gnosis, Philosophy, and the Order of Knowledge* (Bloomington: Indiana University Press, 1988), 17.

31. Du Bois, *The Autobiography of W. E. B. Du Bois,* 143.

32. W. E. B. Du Bois, *The World and Africa: An Inquiry into the Part Which Africa Has Played in World History* (New York: International Publishers, 1981), 35.

33. Ibid.

34. Adam Hochschild, *King Leopold's Ghost: A Story of Greed, Terror, and Heroism in Colonial Africa* (New York: Houghton Mifflin, 1999), 233.

35. Ibid., 225–26.

36. Sven Lindqvist, *"Exterminate All the Brutes": One Man's Odyssey into the Heart of Darkness and the Origins of European Genocide* (trans. Joan Tate; New York: The New Press, 1996), 10.

37. Ibid., 160.

38. Du Bois, *The World and Africa,* 23.

39. Ibid., 17.

40. Ibid., 18.

41. Carl Plasa, *Toni Morrison: Beloved* (New York: Columbia University Press, 1998), 36–37.

42. James Baldwin, *No Name in the Street* (New York: Dell, 1972), 47.

43. Du Bois, *The World and Africa,* 19.

44. Emmanuel Levinas, *Otherwise Than Being: Or Beyond Essence* (Pittsburgh: Duquesne University Press, 2000), 157.

45. Ibid.

46. Ibid.

47. Cullen, "Heritage," 224.

48. Emmanuel Levinas, *Totality and Infinity: An Essay on Exteriority* (Pittsburgh: Duquesne University Press, 1969), 118.
49. Dominique Zahan, *La dialectique du verbe chez les Bambara* (Paris: Mouton, 1963), 9, author's translation.
50. Ibid.
51. Hegel, *The Philosophy of History,* 93.
52. V. Y. Mudimbe, *The Idea of Africa* (Bloomington: Indiana University Press, 1994), 69; emphasis added.
53. Gordon, *Bad Faith and Antiblack Racism,* 149–50.
54. Ibid., 150.
55. Wolfhart Pannenberg, *Theology and the Kingdom of God* (Philadelphia: Westminster Press, 1977), 29; emphasis added.
56. Wolfhart Pannenberg, *Systematic Theology,* vol. 3 (Grand Rapids: Eerdmans, 1998), 620.
57. James Baldwin, *Go Tell It on the Mountain* (New York: Dell, 1985), 200.

Chapter 2: Burning through the Plastic Image: The Approach

1. Levinas, *Totality and Infinity,* 50–51.
2. Du Bois, *The Souls of Black Folk,* 9.
3. Adolf Reed, *W. E. B. Du Bois and American Political Thought: Fabianism and the Color Line* (New York: Oxford University Press, 1997), 107.
4. Ibid., 99.
5. Ibid.
6. Ibid., 175.
7. Hegel, *The Philosophy of History,* 18.
8. Ibid., 49.
9. Ibid.
10. Ibid., 17–18.
11. Du Bois, *The Souls of Black Folk,* 7.
12. Brian Lanker, *I Dream a World: Portraits of Black Women Who Changed America* (New York: Stewart, Tabor and Chang, 1989), 32.
13. Baldwin, *No Name in the Street,* 61.
14. Reed, *W. E. B. Du Bois,* 107.
15. Du Bois, *The Autobiography of W. E. B. Du Bois,* 25.
16. Levinas, *Otherwise Than Being,* 43.
17. Reed, *W. E. B. Du Bois,* 107.
18. Anderson, *Beyond Ontological Blackness,* 14–15, 161.
19. Ibid., 14.
20. Du Bois, *The Souls of Black Folk,* 9, emphasis added.
21. David Levering Lewis, *W. E. B. Du Bois: Biography of a Race, 1968–1919* (New York: Henry Holt, 1993), 282.

22. Du Bois, *Dusk of Dawn,* 32.

23. Du Bois, "The Conservation of Races" in *The Seventh Son: The Thought and Writings of W. E. B. Du Bois,* 2 vols. (ed. Julius Lester; New York: Random House, 1971), 178.

24. Ibid., 177.

25. Levinas, *Otherwise Than Being,* 64.

26. Hegel, *The Philosophy of History,* 15.

27. Ibid., 98.

28. Ibid., 99.

29. Levinas, *Otherwise Than Being,* 187.

30. Du Bois, *The Autobiography of W. E. B. Du Bois,* 17.

31. Ibid.

32. Emmanuel Levinas, *Basic Philosophical Writings* (ed. Adrian T. Peperzak, Simon Critchley, and Robert Bernasconi; Bloomington: Indiana University Press, 1996), 163.

33. Levinas, *Totality and Infinity,* 117.

34. Ibid., 50–51.

35. Levinas, *Otherwise Than Being,* 8.

36. Du Bois, *The Souls of Black Folk,* 5.

37. Levinas, *Totality and Infinity,* 291.

38. Ibid., 258.

39. Levinas, *Otherwise Than Being,* 78.

40. Levinas, *Totality and Infinity,* 78.

41. Claude Meillassoux, *The Anthropology of Slavery: The Womb of Iron and Gold* (Chicago: University of Chicago Press, 1991), 24.

42. Ibid., 28, 32.

43. Ibid., 109.

44. Lewis R. Gordon, *Existentia Africana: Understanding Africana Thought* (New York: Routledge, 2000), 1.

45. Zahan, *The Religion, Spirituality, and Thought of Traditional Africa,* 135–36.

46. Hegel, *The Philosophy of History,* 93.

47. Mudimbe, *The Idea of Africa,* 52; emphasis added.

48. Baldwin, *Go Tell It on the Mountain,* 80–81.

49. Emmanuel Levinas, *Of God Who Comes to Mind* (Stanford: Stanford University Press, 1998), xiv.

50. Ibid.

51. Jürgen Moltmann, *The Coming of God: Christian Eschatology* (Minneapolis: Fortress Press, 1996), 287.

52. Levinas, *Totality and Infinity,* 232.

53. Ibid., 56.

54. Jürgen Moltmann, *The Trinity and the Kingdom: The Doctrine of God* (New York: HarperCollins, 1991), 190.

55. Ibid.

56. Jones, *Is God a White Racist?,* 23.

57. Ibid., 22.
58. Levinas, *Totality and Infinity,* 78.
59. Ibid., 56.
60. Ibid.
61. Ibid.

Chapter 3: "Nobody Knows the Trouble I've Seen": Du Bois's Inner Strength

1. Du Bois, *The Souls of Black Folk,* 201.
2. Du Bois, *Dusk of Dawn,* 98.
3. Du Bois, *The Souls of Black Folk,* 13.
4. Ibid., 9.
5. Du Bois, *Dusk of Dawn,* 115.
6. Ibid., 103.
7. Ibid.
8. W. E. B. Du Bois, *The Negro* (New York: Oxford University Press, 1970), 10.
9. Jared Diamond, *Guns, Germs, and Steel: The Fates of Human Societies* (New York: W. W. Norton, 1999), 25.
10. Du Bois, *The Negro,* 11.
11. Ibid., 12–13.
12. Ibid., 13.
13. Ibid.
14. L. Luca Cavalli-Sforza, Paolo Menozzi, and Alberto Piazza, *The History and Geography of Human Genes* (Princeton: Princeton University Press, 1994), 19.
15. Du Bois, *The Negro,* 82.
16. Ibid.
17. Ibid., 143.
18. Ibid., 90.
19. Kä Mana, *Foi chrétienne, crise africaine et reconstruction de l'Afrique* (Nairobi: CETA, 1992), 25.
20. Ibid.
21. Ivor Wilkes, *Forest of Gold: Essays on the Akan and the Kingdom of the Asante* (Athens: Ohio University Press, 1993), 77.
22. Du Bois, *The Autobiography of W. E. B. Du Bois,* 422.
23. Hegel, *The Philosophy of History,* 323.
24. Levinas, *Totality and Infinity,* 56.
25. Du Bois, *The Souls of Black Folk,* 15.
26. Du Bois, *The Autobiography of W. E. B. Du Bois,* 405.
27. Ibid.
28. Ibid.
29. Du Bois, *Darkwater,* 29.
30. Ibid.

31. Du Bois, *The Autobiography of W. E. B. Du Bois*, 222.
32. Du Bois, *The Souls of Black Folk*, 168.
33. Ibid., 169.
34. Du Bois, *The Autobiography of W. E. B. Du Bois*, 230–31.
35. Ibid.
36. W. E. B. Du Bois, *Black Reconstruction in America, 1860–1880* (New York: Atheneum, 1969), 123–24.
37. Ibid., 124.
38. Ibid., 602.
39. Ibid., 707.
40. Ibid., 634.
41. Ibid., 346–47.

Chapter 4: American Africanism: Toni Morrison's Insight into the Form of God

1. Morrison, *Playing in the Dark*, 90.
2. Ibid., 47.
3. Ibid., xii.
4. Jordan, *White over Black*, 28.
5. Morrison, *Playing in the Dark*, 37–38.
6. Ibid., 7.
7. Ibid., xiii.
8. Levinas, *Of God Who Comes to Mind*, 28.
9. Du Bois, *The Souls of Black Folk*, 11.
10. Toni Morrison, *Beloved* (New York: Alfred A. Knopf, 1987), 163.
11. Ibid., 30.
12. Ibid., 31; emphasis added.
13. Michel Huet, *The Dance, Art and Ritual of Africa* (New York: Pantheon, 1978), 100.
14. Zahan, *La dialectique du verbe chez les Bambara*, 15.
15. Ibid.
16. Ibid., 20.
17. Zahan, *The Religion, Spirituality, and Thought of Traditional Africa*, 135–36.
18. Dominique Zahan, *Sociétés d'initiation Bambara: Le n'domo, le Korè* (Paris: Mouton, 1960), 23.
19. Ibid., 26.
20. Morrison, *Beloved*, 31.
21. Peter Wood, *Black Majority: Negroes in Colonial South Carolina from 1670 through the Stono Rebellion* (New York: W. W. Norton, 1975), 316.
22. Ibid., 326.
23. Morrison, *Beloved*,, 203.
24. Plasa, *Toni Morrison: Beloved*, 31.

25. Sterling Stuckey, *Slave Culture: Nationalist Theory and the Foundations of Black America* (New York: Oxford University Press, 1987), 3–4.

26. Philip Curtin, *The Atlantic Slave Trade: A Census* (Madison: University of Wisconsin Press, 1969), 156.

27. Joseph Holloway, "The Origins of African-American Culture," in *Africanisms in American Culture* (ed. Joseph Holloway; Bloomington: Indiana University Press, 1991), 4.

28. Plasa, *Toni Morrison: Beloved,* 33.

29. Morrison, *Playing in the Dark,* 68.

30. Morrison, *Beloved,* 193.

31. Morrison, *Playing in the Dark,* 50.

32. Morrison, *Beloved,* 198.

33. Ibid., 227.

34. Ibid., 220.

35. Plasa, *Toni Morrison: Beloved,* 147.

36. Morrison, *Beloved,* 88.

37. Ibid., 177.

38. Plasa, *Toni Morrison: Beloved,* 32.

39. Ibid.

40. Ibid., 33.

41. Morrison, *Beloved,* 210.

42. Plasa, *Toni Morrison: Beloved,* 62.

43. Ibid., 63–64.

44. Ibid., 67.

45. Levinas, *Totality and Infinity,* 199.

46. Morrison, *Beloved,* 179.

47. Jones, *Is God a White Racist?,* 23.

48. Morrison, *Beloved,* 275.

49. Levinas, *Of God Who Comes to Mind,* 32.

50. Ibid.

51. Levinas, *Totality and Infinity,* 228.

Chapter 5: God Is Nobody's Toy: James Baldwin's Rejection of a Nullifying Double Standard

1. James Baldwin, *Nobody Knows My Name* (New York: Vintage International, 1993), 136.

2. Levinas, *Of God Who Comes to Mind,* 32.

3. Baldwin, *Nobody Knows My Name,* 136.

4. Levinas, *Of God Who Comes to Mind,* 109.

5. Baldwin, *Go Tell It on the Mountain,* 61.

6. Ibid., 80.

7. Du Bois, *The Souls of Black Folk,* 151.

8. Baldwin, *Go Tell It on the Mountain,* 193.

9. James Baldwin, *The Fire Next Time* (New York: Vintage International, 1993), 29–30.

10. Baldwin, *Go Tell It on the Mountain*, 194.

11. Ibid., 194–95.

12. Ibid., 195.

13. Ibid.

14. Ibid., 196.

15. Ibid., 200.

16. Ibid., 201.

17. Ibid.

18. Ibid., 203–4.

19. Ibid., 204.

20. James Baldwin, *The Devil Finds Work* (New York: Dell, 1976), 137–38.

21. Baldwin, *The Fire Next Time*, 31.

22. Ibid.

23. Ibid., 38–39.

24. Ibid., 33.

25. Baldwin, *The Devil Finds Work*, 138.

26. Du Bois, *The Souls of Black Folk*, 155.

27. Baldwin, *The Fire Next Time*, 31.

28. Ibid., 40–41.

29. Emmanuel Levinas, *Alterity and Transcendence* (New York: Columbia University Press, 1999), 95.

30. Baldwin, *The Fire Next Time*, 47.

31. Baldwin, *Nobody Knows My Name*, 32.

32. Ibid., 79, 81.

33. Baldwin, *Notes of a Native Son*, xiv.

34. Ivor Wilkes, *Asante in the Nineteenth Century* (Cambridge: Cambridge University Press, 1975), 679–80.

35. David Leeming, *James Baldwin: A Biography* (New York: Alfred A. Knopf, 1994), 208.

36. Ibid.

37. Baldwin, *No Name in the Street*, 49.

38. Ibid., 192.

39. Ibid.

40. Ibid., 193.

41. Ibid.

42. Ibid.

43. Baldwin, *Nobody Knows My Name*, 136.

Chapter 6: Questions Louder Than Drums: This Discomfort

1. Baldwin, *No Name in the Street*, 193.

2. Ibid.

3. Ibid., 194.

4. Wole Soyinka, *The Burden of Memory, the Muse of Forgiveness* (New York: Oxford University Press, 1999), 59.

5. Ibid.

6. Ibid., 69.

7. Ibid., 48.

8. Ibid., 49.

9. Ibid., 48.

10. Ibid., 64–65.

11. Baldwin, *No Name in the Street*, 193.

12. Soyinka, *Burden of Memory*, 52.

13. Baldwin, *No Name in the Street*, 194.

14. Soyinka, *Burden of Memory*, 48.

15. Ibid., 62.

16. Ibid., 62–63.

17. Evans Zuesse, *Ritual Cosmos: The Sanctification of Life in African Religions* (Athens: Ohio University Press, 1979), 123.

18. Luc de Heusch, *Sacrifice in Africa: A Structuralist Approach* (Bloomington: Indiana University Press, 1985), 98.

19. Ibid., 98–99.

20. Ibid., 98.

21. Ibid., 29.

22. Ibid.

23. Ibid., 37.

24. Ibid.

25. Ibid., 29.

26. Ibid., 124.

27. Ibid., 37.

28. Ibid., 36.

29. Meillassoux, *The Anthropology of Slavery*, 180.

30. Ibid.

31. Ibid.

32. Ibid.

33. Ibid.

34. Soyinka, *Burden of Memory*, 54.

35. Chinua Achebe, *Hopes and Impediments* (New York: Anchor Books/Doubleday, 1989), 45.

36. R. S. Rattray, *Religion and Art in Ashanti* (London: Oxford University Press, 1927), 26.

37. Ibid.

38. Ibid., 23.

39. Ibid.

40. Wilkes, *Forest of Gold*, 44.

41. Ibid., 43–44.

42. Mana, *Foi chrétienne*, 68, author's translation.

43. Baldwin, *No Name in the Street,* 194.
44. Hegel, *The Philosophy of History,* 99.

Chapter 7: From Ryangombe the Blood Pact to the Bloody Panga

1. Baldwin, *No Name in the Street,* 193.
2. Keith Richburg, *Out of America: A Black Man Confronts Africa* (New York: Basic Books/HarperCollins, 1997), 15–16.
3. Ibid., 18.
4. Ibid., 20.
5. Ibid., ix.
6. Ibid., xii.
7. Ibid., xiv.
8. Gérard Prunier, *The Rwanda Crisis: History of a Genocide* (New York: Columbia University Press, 1997), 5, emphasis added.
9. J. J. Maquet, "The Kingdom of Rwanda," in *African Worlds: Studies in the Cosmological Ideas and Social Values of African Peoples* (ed. Daryll Forde; New York: Oxford University Press, 1976), 164–65.
10. Ibid.,185.
11. de Heusch, *Sacrifice in Africa,* 117.
12. Maquet, "The Kingdom of Rwanda," 171.
13. Vincent Mulago, "Le pacte du sang et la communion alimentaire: Pierres d'attente de la communion eucharistique," in *Des prêtres noirs s'interrogent* (Paris: Les éditions du Cerf, 1956), 173–76.
14. Ibid., 176.
15. Prunier, *The Rwanda Crisis,* 6–7.
16. Ibid., 8.
17. Ibid., 9.
18. Philip Gourevitch, *We Wish to Inform You That Tomorrow We Will Be Killed with Our Families: Stories from Rwanda* (New York: Farrar, Straus and Giroux, 1999), 56–57.
19. Fergal Keane, *Season of Blood: A Rwandan Journey* (New York: Penguin, 1995), 17.
20. Prunier, *The Rwanda Crisis,* 19.
21. Ibid., 21.
22. Ibid., 22.
23. Richburg, *Out of America,* 103.
24. Prunier, *The Rwanda Crisis,* 32.
25. Ibid., 34.
26. Ibid.
27. Ibid., 35.
28. Gourevitch, *We Wish to Inform You,* 58.
29. Prunier, *The Rwanda Crisis,* 54.
30. Keane, *Season of Blood,* 18–19.

31. Prunier, *The Rwanda Crisis*, 238.
32. Richburg, *Out of America*, 247.
33. Baldwin, *No Name in the Street*, 193.
34. Richburg, *Out of America*, 109–10.
35. Hegel, *The Philosophy of History*, 99.
36. Richburg, *Out of America*, xiv.
37. Hegel, *The Philosophy of History*, 99.

Chapter 8: *Une surprenante analogie:* Reinvesting Christian Symbols with Their Original Energy

1. Baldwin, *The Devil Finds Work*, 138.
2. Baldwin, *No Name in the Street*, 193–94.
3. Ibid., 194.
4. Ibid., 49.
5. Ibid.
6. Ibid.
7. Ibid.
8. Sigmund Freud, *Beyond the Pleasure Principle* (New York: W. W. Norton, 1989), 46–49.
9. Hegel, *The Philosophy of History*, 33.
10. Levinas, *Totality and Infinity*, 272.
11. Ibid., 273.
12. Levinas, *Otherwise Than Being*, 74, 78.
13. Mulago, "Le pacte du sang et la communion alimentaire," 179.
14. Ibid.
15. Ibid., 177.
16. Georg Wilhelm Friedrich Hegel, *Lectures on the Philosophy of Religion* (Berkeley: University of California, 1988), 231.
17. Ibid.
18. Hegel, *The Philosophy of History*, 93.
19. V. Y. Mudimbe, *Tales of Faith: Religion as Political Performance in Central Africa* (Atlantic Highlands, N.J.: Athlone Press, 1997), 90–92.
20. Ibid., 92.
21. Ibid.
22. Ibid.
23. Ibid., 148.
24. Ibid., 151.
25. Ibid., 95.
26. Mulago, "Le pacte du sang," 180–81, author's translation.
27. Ibid., 186–87.
28. Ibid., 183, author's translation.
29. Richard Bjornson, *The African Quest for Freedom and Identity* (Bloomington: Indiana University Press, 1994), 139.
30. Ibid., 143.

31. Engelbert Mveng, *L'art d'Afrique noire: Liturgie cosmique et langage religieux* (Yaounde: Éditions CLE, 1974), 6.
32. Ibid.
33. Ibid.
34. Ibid., 7.
35. Ibid., 24, author's translation.
36. Ibid., 29.
37. Ibid., 30.
38. Ibid., 30–31.
39. Ibid., 31.
40. Ibid., 34, author's translation.
41. Ibid., 73.
42. Ibid., 76.
43. Ibid.
44. Ibid.
45. Ibid.
46. Ibid.
47. Ibid., 100.
48. Ibid.
49. Ibid., 121, author's translation.
50. Ibid., 45, author's translation.
51. Meillassoux, *The Anthropology of Slavery,* 78.
52. Ibid., 160.
53. Ibid., 168.
54. Ibid., 207.
55. Ibid.
56. Mveng, *L'art d'Afrique noire,* 122.

Chapter 9: The Mysterious Love of a Third-Party God

1. Baldwin, *Go Tell It on the Mountain,* 80–81; emphasis added.
2. James Baldwin, "White Racisim or World Community," in *The Price of the Ticket* (New York: St. Martin's/Marek, 1985), 435.
3. Baldwin, *Nobody Knows My Name,* 136.
4. Dietrich Bonhoeffer, *Creation and Fall* (Minneapolis: Fortress Press, 1997), 30.
5. Ibid., 35.
6. Ibid., 27.
7. Ibid., 28.
8. Jürgen Moltmann, *God in Creation* (Minneapolis: Fortress Press, 1993), 87.
9. Moltmann, *The Coming of God,* 299.
10. Engelbert Mveng, "Récent développements de la théologie africaine," in *Bulletin de théologie africaine 5,* no. 9 (January–June 1983): 141.

11. Ibid., 142, author's translation.

12. Engelbert Mveng, "Third World Theology — What Theology? What Third World?," in *Irruption of the Third World: Challenge to Theology.* (ed. Virginia Fabella and Sergio Torres; Maryknoll, N.Y.: Orbis Books, 1983), 220.

13. Engelbert Mveng, "A Cultural Perspective," in *Doing Theology in a Divided World* (ed. Virginia Fabella and Sergio Torres; Maryknoll, N.Y.: Orbis Books, 1985), 72.

14. Ludwig Feuerbach, *The Essence of Christianity* (Amherst, N.Y.: Prometheus, 1989), 56.

15. Ibid., 137.

16. Ibid., 138; emphasis added.

17. Moltmann, *The Crucified God*, 251.

18. Feuerbach, *The Essence of Christianity*, 53.

19. Ibid.

20. Jürgen Moltmann, *Experiences in Theology: Ways and Forms of Christian Theology* (Minneapolis: Fortress Press, 2000), 58.

21. Du Bois, *The Autobiography of W. E. B. Du Bois*, 422–23.

22. Morrison, *Beloved*, 30.

23. Baldwin, *Nobody Knows My Name*, xiv.

Bibliography

Achebe, Chinua. *Hopes and Impediments*. New York: Anchor Books/ Doubleday, 1989.

Anderson, Victor. *Beyond Ontological Blackness: An Essay on African American Religious and Cultural Criticism*. New York: Continuum, 1995.

Baldwin, James. *The Fire Next Time*. New York: Vintage International, 1993.

———. *Nobody Knows My Name*. New York: Vintage International, 1993.

———. *The Price of the Ticket*. New York: St. Martin's/Marek, 1985.

———. *Go Tell It on the Mountain*. New York: Dell, 1985.

———. *Notes of a Native Son*. Boston: Beacon Press, 1984.

———. *The Devil Finds Work*. New York: Dell, 1976.

———. *No Name in the Street*. New York: Dell, 1972.

Bjornson, Richard. *The African Quest for Freedom and Identity*. Bloomington: Indiana University Press, 1994.

Bonhoeffer, Dietrich. *Creation and Fall*. Minneapolis: Fortress Press, 1997.

Cavalli-Sforza, L. Luca, Paolo Menozzi, and Alberto Piazza. *The History and Geography of Human Genes*. Princeton: Princeton University Press, 1994.

Cullen, Countee. "Heritage." In *The Book of Negro Poetry*. Edited by James Weldon Johnson. New York: Harcourt, Brace, and World, 1958.

Curtin, Philip. *The Atlantic Slave Trade: A Census*. Madison: University of Wisconsin Press, 1969.

de Heusch, Luc. *Sacrifice in Africa: A Structuralist Approach*. Bloomington: Indiana University Press, 1985.

Diamond, Jared. *Guns, Germs, and Steel: The Fates of Human Societies*. New York: W. W. Norton, 1999.

Du Bois, W. E. B. *The Souls of Black Folk*. New York: Alfred A. Knopf, 1993.

———. *The Autobiography of W. E. B. Du Bois: A Soliloquy on Viewing My Life from the Last Decade of Its First Century*. New York: International Publishers, 1991.

———. *Dusk of Dawn: An Essay toward an Autobiography of a Race Concept*. New Brunswick, N.J.: Transaction Books, 1984.

―――. *The World and Africa: An Inquiry into the Part Which Africa Has Played in World History.* New York: International Publishers, 1981.

―――. *Darkwater: Voices from within the Veil.* Millwood, N.Y.: Kraus-Thompson, 1975.

―――. "The Conservation of Races." In *The Seventh Son: The Thought and Writings of W. E. B. Du Bois.* 2 vols. Edited by Julius Lester. New York: Random House, 1971.

―――. *The Negro.* New York: Oxford University Press, 1970.

―――. *The Suppression of the African Slave-Trade to the United States of America, 1638–1870.* Mineola, N.Y.: Dover Publications, 1970.

―――. *Black Reconstruction in America, 1860–1880.* New York: Atheneum, 1969.

Feuerbach, Ludwig. *The Essence of Christianity.* Amherst, N.Y.: Prometheus Books, 1989.

Freud, Sigmund. *Beyond the Pleasure Principle.* New York: W. W. Norton, 1989.

Gordon, Lewis R. *Existentia Africana: Understanding Africana Thought.* New York: Routledge, 2000.

―――. *Bad Faith and Antiblack Racism.* Atlantic Highlands, N.J.: Humanities Press, 1995.

Gourevitch, Philip. *We Wish to Inform You That Tomorrow We Will Be Killed with Our Families: Stories from Rwanda.* New York: Farrar Straus and Giroux, 1999.

Hegel, Georg Wilhelm Friedrich. *Philosophy of Mind.* New York: Oxford University Press, 1990.

―――. *Lectures on the Philosophy of Religion.* Berkeley: University of California Press, 1988.

―――. *The Philosophy of History.* New York: Dover, 1956.

Hochschild, Adam. *King Leopold's Ghost: A Story of Greed, Terror, and Heroism in Colonial Africa.* New York: Houghton Mifflin, 1999.

Holloway, Joseph, ed., *Africanisms in American Culture.* Bloomington: Indiana University Press, 1991.

Huet, Michel. *The Dance, Art and Ritual of Africa.* New York: Pantheon, 1978.

Jones, William. *Is God a White Racist? A Preamble to Black Theology.* Boston: Beacon Press , 1998.

Jordan, Winthrop. *White over Black: American Attitudes toward the Negro, 1550–1812.* New York: W. W. Norton, 1977.

Keane, Fergal. *Season of Blood: A Rwandan Journey.* New York: Penguin, 1995.

Lanker, Brian. *I Dream a World: Portraits of Black Women Who Changed America.* New York: Stewart, Tabor and Chang, 1989.

Leeming, David. *James Baldwin: A Biography.* New York: Alfred A. Knopf, 1994.

Levinas, Emmanuel. *Otherwise Than Being: Or Beyond Essence.* Pittsburgh: Duquesne University Press, 2000.

———. *Alterity and Transcendence.* New York: Columbia University Press, 1999.

———. *Of God Who Comes to Mind.* Stanford: Stanford University Press, 1998.

———. *Basic Philosophical Writings.* Edited by Adrian T. Peperzak, Simon Critchley, and Robert Bernasconi. Bloomington: Indiana University Press, 1996.

———. *Outside the Subject.* Stanford: Stanford University Press, 1994.

———. *Totality and Infinity: An Essay on Exteriority.* Pittsburgh: Duquesne University Press, 1969.

Lewis, David Levering. *W. E. B. Du Bois: Biography of a Race, 1968–1919.* New York: Henry Holt, 1993.

Lindqvist, Sven. *"Exterminate All the Brutes": One Man's Odyssey into the Heart of Darkness and the Origins of European Genocide.* Translated by Joan Tate. New York: The New Press, 1996.

Mana, Kä. *Christ d'Afrique: Enjeux éthiques de la foi africaine en Jésus-Christ.* Paris: Karthala, 1994.

———. *Foi chrétienne, crise africaine et reconstruction de l'Afrique.* Nairobi: CETA, 1992.

Maquet, J. J. "The Kingdom of Rwanda." In *African Worlds: Studies in the Cosmological Ideas and Social Values of African Peoples.* Edited by Daryll Forde. New York: Oxford University Press, 1976.

Meillassoux, Claude. *The Anthropology of Slavery: The Womb of Iron and Gold.* Chicago: University of Chicago Press, 1991.

Moltmann, Jürgen. *Experiences in Theology: Ways and Forms of Christian Theology.* Minneapolis: Fortress Press, 2000.

———. *The Coming of God: Christian Eschatology.* Minneapolis: Fortress Press, 1996.

———. *God in Creation.* Minneapolis: Fortress Press, 1993.

———. *The Crucified God: The Cross as the Foundation and Criticism of Christian Theology.* Minneapolis: Fortress Press, 1993.

———. *The Way of Jesus Christ: Christology in Messianic Dimensions.* Minneapolis: Fortress Press, 1993.

———. *The Trinity and the Kingdom: The Doctrine of God.* New York: HarperCollins, 1991.

———. "Introduction." *Union Seminary Quarterly Review* 31, no. 1 (fall 1975): 3–4.

Morrison, Toni. *Playing in the Dark: Whiteness and the Literary Imagination.* Cambridge: Harvard University Press, 1992.

———. *Beloved.* New York: Alfred A. Knopf, 1987.

Mudimbe, V. Y. *Tales of Faith: Religion as Political Performance in Central Africa.* Atlantic Highlands, N.J.: Athlone Press, 1997.

———. *The Idea of Africa.* Bloomington: Indiana University Press, 1994.

———. *The Invention of Africa: Gnosis, Philosophy, and the Order of Knowledge.* Bloomington: Indiana University Press, 1988.

Mulago, Vincent. "Le pacte du sang et la communion alimentaire: Pierres d'attente de la communion eucharistique." In *Des prêtres noirs s'interrogent*. Paris: Les éditions du Cerf, 1956.

Mveng, Engelbert. "A Cultural Perspective." In *Doing Theology in a Divided World*. Edited by Virginia Fabella and Sergio Torres. Maryknoll, N.Y.: Orbis Books, 1985.

———. "Third World Theology — What Theology? What Third World?" In *Irruption of the Third World: Challenge to Theology*. Edited by Virginia Fabella and Sergio Torres. Maryknoll, N.Y.: Orbis Books, 1983.

———. "Récent développements de la théologie africaine." *Bulletin de théologie africaine* 5, no. 9 (January–June 1983): 137–44.

———. *L'art d'Afrique noire: Liturgie cosmique et langage religieux*. Yaounde: Éditions CLE, 1974.

Pannenberg, Wolfhart. *Systematic Theology*. Vol. 3. Grand Rapids: Eerdmans, 1998.

———. *Theology and the Kingdom of God* Philadelphia: Westminster Press, 1977.

Pinn, Anthony. *Why Lord? Suffering and Evil in Black Theology*. New York: Continuum, 1995.

Plasa, Carl. *Toni Morrison: Beloved*. New York: Columbia University Press, 1998.

Prunier, Gérard. *The Rwanda Crisis: History of a Genocide*. New York: Columbia University Press, 1997.

Rattray, R. S. *Religion and Art in Ashanti*. London: Oxford University Press, 1927.

Reed, Adolf. *W. E. B. Du Bois and American Political Thought: Fabianism and the Color Line*. New York: Oxford University Press, 1997.

Richburg, Keith. *Out of America: A Black Man Confronts Africa*. New York: Basic Books/HarperCollins, 1997.

Soyinka, Wole. *The Burden of Memory, the Muse of Forgiveness*. New York: Oxford University Press, 1999.

Stuckey, Sterling. *Slave Culture: Nationalist Theory and the Foundations of Black America*. New York: Oxford University Press, 1987.

Wilkes, Ivor. *Forest of Gold: Essays on the Akan and the Kingdom of the Asante*. Athens: Ohio University Press, 1993.

———. *Asante in the Nineteenth Century*. Cambridge: Cambridge University Press, 1975.

Wood, Peter. *Black Majority: Negroes in Colonial South Carolina from 1670 through the Stono Rebellion*. New York: W. W. Norton, 1975.

Zahan, Dominique. *The Religion, Spirituality, and Thought of Traditional Africa*. Chicago: University of Chicago Press, 1983.

———. *La dialectique du verbe chez les Bambara*. Paris: Mouton, 1963.

———. *Sociétés d'initiation Bambara: Le n'domo, le Korè*. Paris: Mouton, 1960.

Zuesse, Evans. *Ritual Cosmos: The Sanctification of Life in African Religions*. Athens: Ohio University Press, 1979.

Index

Achebe, Chinua, 76
Africana spirituality
    and antelope dance, 25, 26
    and black essayist and novelists, 30
    and definition of Africana thought
      (Gordon), 49
    as dogged strength, 31
    and Engelbert Mveng, 96
    and the mysterious love of God, 27
    and traces of the ancestors, 108
Anderson, Victor, 17
    and critique of double-consciousness,
      20–22
    on ontological blackness, 5
antelope dance, 25, 26, 50, 52, 62, 102
    Sethe's memory of, 50
Atlanta University, 41

Baldwin, James
    on African roots of the black
      American church, 61–62
    on black-white "friendship," 19
    on Christianization of African exile,
      5
    on the dark gods, 65, 69, 91
    The Devil Finds Work, 60
    and double-consciousness, 65
    "East River, Downtown," 63
    "Everybody's Protest Novel," 5
    experience in Africa, 64–65
    on fecundity and sterility, 65–66, 69
    The Fire Next Time, 57–58, 61
    Go Tell it on the Mountain, 27, 31,
      57–58, 103
    as John Grimes, 27
    and Mount Calvary of the Pentecostal
      Faith, 57
    Nobody Knows My Name, 63
    Notes of a Native Son, 64
    "Princes and Powers," 63
    relationship to Mother Horn, 57
    threshing-floor experience of, 58–61,
      103–4
    and the white God, 61
    "White Racism or World
      Community," 104

Baldwin, William, 42
Bambara
    and the antelope dance, 47
    divinities of, 48
    relation to South Carolina, 51
    on the spiritual character of the
      human body, 48
    and the theistic significance of the
      word, 13, 48
    on the *Tyiwara,* 48–49
    Zahan on, 13
Beloved (Morrison)
    Africanist characters, 52–54
    and the antelope dance, 25, 47, 50,
      52, 108
    Baby Suggs's *aporia* and exhaustion
      in, 55
    and the Bambara, 47, 50
    and Civil War, 46
    and the little antelope, 47
    and the Middle Passage, 47, 53–54
    and "Of Our Spiritual Strivings,"
      46
    and Reconstruction, 46
    and schoolteacher, 51
    and Sethe's escape, 50
    and the *Tyiwara,* 52
Berlin Conference, 9
Black theology, 5
Bonhoeffer, Dietrich
    Creation and Fall, 104
    on the new creation, 104
    opposition to Hegel's philosophy,
      104

Christianity
    and African religion, 94
    and Africana spirituality, 27
    imposition on African people, 3
    as the Religion, 3
    and "slave humanity," 70
    and traditional religionists, 79
    as universal history, 8
    as Whiteanity, 4, 8
    as the white man's religion, 4, 7